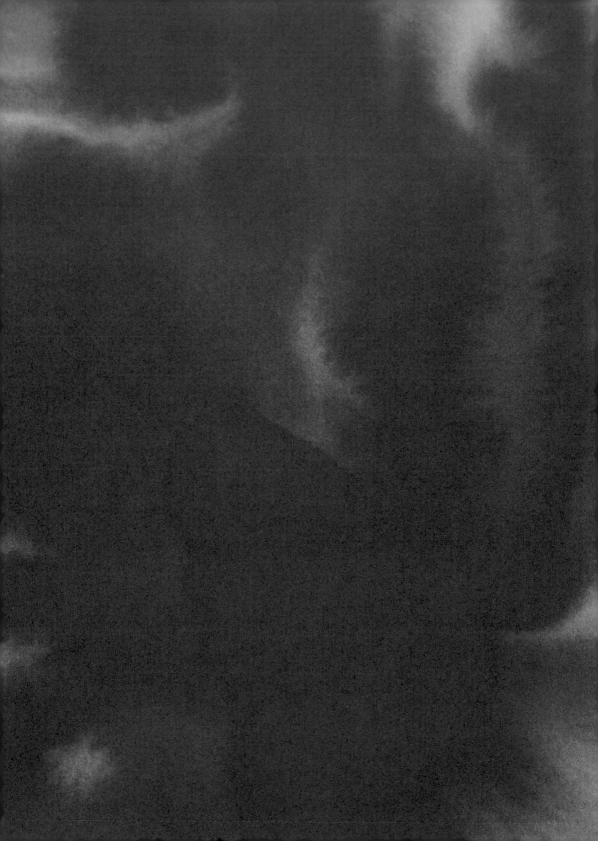

EVERYDAY
TAROT

This book is dedicated to YOU.
To your soul essence,
your inner wisdom,
and your infinite potential.
Anything is possible.

EVERYDAY
TAROT

UNLOCK YOUR INNER WISDOM
AND MANIFEST YOUR FUTURE

BRIGIT ESSELMONT
founder of **BIDDY TAROT**

illustrations by
ELEANOR GROSCH

Running Press
PHILADELPHIA

Running Press
Hachette Book Group
1290 Avenue of the Americas, New York, NY 10104
www.runningpress.com
@Running_Press

Printed in Canada

Published by Running Press, an imprint of Perseus Books, LLC, a subsidiary of Hachette Book Group, Inc. The Running Press name and logo is a trademark of the Hachette Book Group.

The Hachette Speakers Bureau provides a wide range of authors for speaking events. To find out more, go to www.hachettespeakersbureau.com or call (866) 376-6591.

The publisher is not responsible for websites (or their content) that are not owned by the publisher.

Print book cover and interior design by Susan Van Horn

Library of Congress Control Number: 2018944323

ISBNs: 978-0-7624-9280-0 (hardcover),
978-0-7624-9278-7 (ebook)

FRI

10 9 8 7 6 5 4

CONTENTS

• ✴ ✦ ✴ •

INTRODUCTION

FOUR A.M. IT WAS PITCH BLACK OUTSIDE, AND THE AIR WAS COLD. I was wide awake.

I was fourteen years old and on a mission to master the art of ESP, extrasensory perception. So, I lit a candle and stared into the flame. The minutes ticked past as I stared and stared. Five minutes. Ten. Twenty. I sat there just waiting for something "extrasensory" to happen. But all I saw was the flickering flame in front of me.

I opened my tattered ESP book, a hand-me-down from my mother, and reread the page outlining what I could *expect* to happen when I stared at the flame. My third eye would open, the book promised, and I'd receive infinite wisdom from the Universe. *Oh dear.* All I got was a headache and a black spot in front of my eyes.

Candle gazing wasn't the only thing I tried to increase my psychic abilities. I made my own Zener ESP cards—five cardboard cards with different shapes and colors—and did my best to switch on my supernatural powers to guess what was on each card as they lay facedown in front of me.

But alas, I only got a 20 percent hit rate and a growing feeling I was not a born psychic.

So, I gave up on ESP and instead focused on all kinds of spirituality and religion. I learned about Christianity, Buddhism, Taoism, Hinduism, Judaism, and Islam (thanks to the open-minded religious education teacher at my Presbyterian school). And I delved into Wicca, Paganism, and witchcraft (hey, *The Craft* came out when I was in high school!). I experimented with spell crafting, meditation, yoga, prayer, chanting, and more gazing, this time at sacred symbols like Om and the Flower of Life.

The timing was perfect. My high school years were rocky, dealing with the usual issues of troubled friendships, nasty bullies, and broken hearts as I experienced love (and lust) for the first time. Exploring these different spiritual systems helped to keep me grounded and open-minded as I discovered new aspects of myself and how I fit into the world.

In 1997, when I was seventeen, I traveled to Germany as a high school exchange student. I was keen to become fluent in German and expand my horizons in a new culture. I went to see a Tarot card reader before I left, just as a bit of fun, to see what might happen on this six-month trip. The reader was in an old part of town with a painted wooden sign out front. I walked up the creaky wooden stairs, through a purple and gold sheer curtain, and into a small room filled with crystals, angelic statues, incense smoke, and, of course, Tarot cards. It was like walking into a movie set, and I wondered if this was part of the act.

The woman invited me to sit down, then reached out and held my hands. "What do you want to know, dear?" she asked, her eyes piercing into my soul, reading every thought I had—or, so I feared. I explained I was going abroad for six months and wanted to find out what might happen when I got there. She picked up her well-loved cards and, closing her eyes, mumbled something to herself then shuffled. Meanwhile, my heart was racing and my palms were sweating, as I looked for the nearest exit in case she flew around the room. The woman opened her eyes and then peeled off the top card of the deck, laying it down on the table.

"Ooh, the Emperor! You're going to find love in Germany, doll. Real love. Not all that high school stuff you've been contending with. Your heart will open in a big way, and you'll fall madly in love with a sweetheart."

For a moment, I was super-excited. Love? That sounded amazing! But then the doubt and skepticism rushed in. *I bet she says this to everyone. She's just telling me what I want to hear. This isn't real. This is BS.*

I walked away from the reading thinking I had just wasted my fifty bucks on someone who made up whatever her clients yearned to hear. But there was also a part of me that was hopeful—sneakingly optimistic that what she had said was right and I would find love. "Oh, stop dreaming!" my mind kept telling me. So I forgot about the reading and moved on with practicing my German and getting ready for the big trip.

I was in love six months later. I had found the boy of my dreams, a real sweetheart who wanted to impress me and take care of me. We met in class at the local high school, and he was keen to show me around and give me a taste of the German lifestyle.

Later, he invited me to stay at his home for a few weeks when I had a falling out with my host family. It was a blissful romance that came to its inevitable end when my six months were up and I had to fly home to Australia. There were tears and promises to stay in touch, but, eventually and inevitably, we grew apart– although, his mum still sends us gifts every year and emails with regular updates.

The Tarot reader was right. He was my first Emperor!

That got me thinking. If the Tarot cards predicted this new romance, then surely they could do so much more. So I asked my parents for a deck of cards for Christmas, and I learned how to read Tarot.

LEARNING TAROT—THE EARLY DAYS

At first, I was keen to learn how to use the Tarot cards to predict the future, just as the woman had done for my first reading.

As a diligent first-year university student studying commerce and arts, I did what had worked for me throughout my education. I created a study plan and set about memorizing the card meanings, rote learning how to do a Tarot reading.

I bought a dozen books on Tarot cards, created my own notebook with a few blank pages set aside for each card, and scheduled at least one hour a day to study. I decided to start with the Fool—the first card in the deck—and move my way through each of the seventy-eight Tarot cards, until I knew every single meaning by heart. Then, I would be a master of Tarot—or so I thought.

Off I went—spending hours reading about each card, taking copious amounts of notes, and then doing spot quizzes to make sure I had remembered what I learned about them all.

Then I learned how to do a Tarot reading. I researched what I would need for a reading (a cloth, crystals, candles, essential oils, and so on), learned the techniques for shuffling and laying out the cards, and memorized the most popular Tarot spreads.

Eventually, I felt ready to do my first "real" Tarot reading! Hoping to gain insight into my love life, I asked, "When will I find love?" and shuffled the cards, laying them in the ten-card Celtic Cross (purportedly *the* spread for reading Tarot). The first card represented me in my present situation—the Page of Cups, with a young man holding a cup with a fish jumping over the rim. I scanned my memory bank and remembered, "Ah! A message or invitation! A surprise that brings joy." Things sounded good so far.

Then I looked at the second card, representing the challenge—the Nine of Swords, where a woman has awoken from a nightmare and is holding her head in her hands. "Oh dear. Worry, anxiety, nightmares," I recalled. And so the reading went on.

By the end of the reading, I had ten different messages about my future love life from the ten different cards. It was interesting, but not the massive download from the Universe I had been hoping for. And it was a little confusing, to be honest. Every card had its own message and nothing fit together into a broader message. Plus, every book had a slightly different meaning for the cards, and I was never sure which was the "right" one.

I kept practicing like this for a year or two, hoping that over time I would someday master the Tarot and be able to predict the future with my new superpowers.

It didn't quite turn out the way I wanted. Every reading felt robotic. Instead of opening my third eye and accessing the psychic realm, I was busy trying to remember what the cards meant, hoping I was right. Maybe I wasn't cut out for this.

I put my Tarot cards in the back of a drawer, feeling disappointed and upset that I had just spent two years trying to learn how to read but still couldn't do what I wanted. Fortune-telling would just have to wait for a different lifetime.

A few months later, I got a niggling feeling I needed to reconnect with my Tarot cards again. So one morning, I dug them out and lay them in front of me. I knew from my earlier work that rote learning just wasn't cutting it. So this time, I tried something different.

I shuffled the deck and pulled a card: the High Priestess. This time, instead of trying to recall its precise meaning, I let myself gaze at the imagery of the card and allowed myself to "drink" it all in. The beautiful woman had a dreamy, all-knowing vibe about her. The crescent near her feet reminded me of the wise, feminine energy of the moon. Then I saw the pillars on either side and sensed she was the guardian of a sacred space, and I remembered that there were pillars in some

other cards, like Justice and the Hierophant. I wondered, "Is there a connection there?" Then I saw the book in her lap, as if she had all the answers to life's questions at her fingertips, and also inside her mind and heart.

I felt something shift within me as I gazed at this card. My mind was no longer in overdrive, fretting about the "right" meaning. Instead, a beautiful energy flowed over me, and I could feel my own sense of knowing, just like the High Priestess. Then it dawned on me: the High Priestess was . . . me. *I was the High Priestess.* I closed my eyes and imagined myself as this woman, sitting in this sacred space, with all the answers I needed available to me. I understood that I, not some Tarot book or expert authority, was the source of all knowledge. Everything was within me.

With this powerful insight, I started reading Tarot differently. Instead of *thinking* what a card meant, I *felt* what it meant to me. Instead of worrying about the right meaning for a card, I let the imagery and symbolism of the card guide me. And what happened was magical. I established a personal and intuitive connection with the Tarot cards and, ultimately, a personal and intuitive connection with *myself*.

When I operated this way, my readings were so much more in the "flow." I could see the story. It wasn't about piecing together individual card meanings, but instead beautiful, intuitive connections were coming through the cards, creating a personalized and relevant narrative. Rather than using the cards for fortune-telling and party tricks, I saw the lusciousness of the insights I could attain from them, perspectives that showed me more about the present moment and my true potential. A whole new world was opening up to me in a beautiful and unique way.

And as a result, I discovered that I *was* intuitive and I gained a deeper appreciation of my own spirituality. I trusted myself more, and as I read for more and more people, my client interactions became much more enriching.

I had finally discovered that blissful place where Tarot *flows*, and I was ready to share it.

THE BIRTH OF BIDDY TAROT

While I was learning to read Tarot back in 1999, I also started my own website to share what I was finding out about the cards with others on the Internet (and let's be honest, I needed the distraction from studying accounting and economics). Every time I uncovered something new, I would post it to my website—Tarot card meanings and spreads, techniques, you name it. By 2001, I was offering ten-card Tarot readings for ten dollars (crazy cheap, right?), and people bought them!

I didn't realize it then, but this fun side hobby would later turn into the seven-figure business people now know as Biddy Tarot.

WHY "BIDDY" TAROT?

Many people ask me, "What does the 'Biddy' mean?" Well, I wish I had an impressive story to tell you about how I meditated in the rainforest about my business name and dreamed of a cute, furry kangaroo that whispered the words, "Biddy Tarot."

But alas, it wouldn't be the truth.

In fact, the truth is a little embarrassing.

When I was thirteen, *all* my friends had cool nicknames—except me.

So I did what any kid would do: I made up my own nickname—Biddy (short for Brigit)—and encouraged everyone to call me by it.

The only problem was . . . my plan didn't work.

Everyone kept calling me Brigit, much to my disappointment, and I had to give up on ever having a nickname.

Seven years later, I was gearing up to launch my website and to begin my professional Tarot reading practice, but I didn't feel comfortable using my real name. So out came "Biddy," and Biddy Tarot was born!

Now, twenty years later, Biddy Tarot has blossomed into the leading online learning community for people who read Tarot. Every year, Biddy Tarot helps over four million people read Tarot and is consistently in the top rankings on Google as a trusted source for card meanings and tutorials. Over 2,000 students have taken part in our online training courses, and we have more than 1,000 members in our Biddy Tarot Community. We employ fifteen team members (including my husband) and now generate an annual revenue of over $1 million through our online courses, books, audio programs, and a membership site.

It seriously blows my mind.

Thanks to the success of the Biddy Tarot business, I can spend more time at home with my family; I've manifested my dream home on the Sunshine Coast, Australia; we live an abundant lifestyle; and we can travel regularly and take extended breaks to do fun things together.

At the same time, Biddy Tarot is giving me the space to go deeper with my own spiritual practice. And every time I teach others about Tarot, I end up teaching myself something new too. It nudges me along, inviting me to go deeper.

It is more than I ever could have hoped that day as I gazed at the High Priestess and read the Tarot *intuitively* for the first time.

HOW I USE TAROT NOW

When I started learning Tarot, I focused on mastering the Tarot card meanings and reading with confidence. My goal was to do a Tarot reading from start to finish, without going blank or worrying whether I had it right, and to create an accurate and insightful reading using the cards and my intuition.

I then put my energy and attention into reading Tarot for others, as a professional reader. Over twenty years I read for over ten-thousand clients, mostly online. Now, you would think having read for thousands of clients, I would have "mastered" Tarot, but what I came to realize is that you can never fully do that. It's an ongoing journey where you reconnect with your inner wisdom. The deeper you go with the Tarot, the deeper you go with yourself. My epiphany fundamentally changed my practice.

In fact, in the last two years, I have moved away from reading Tarot for others and am now focusing on teaching people how to read their own Tarot cards and connect with their own intuition. You see, I believe it is so much more powerful when you *discover* the answers rather than have them read to you by someone else.

I noticed it in my own practice. Yes, I could help other people create significant transformations in their lives. However, I had the most impact when I read Tarot for myself and when I taught others to do the same. And so my Tarot practice evolved into something personal and private. I use Tarot throughout my day to support myself in reflecting on the present moment and connecting with my inner wisdom.

While many people go straight to the Tarot cards, I go to my intuition first through meditation, breathing, visualization, and deep listening—only *then* do I consult the cards. This shifts the energy from depending on my cards to relying on my intuition and inner wisdom and using the cards as a way to deepen my connection with my Higher Self.

I'll share more about what happens when you read Tarot intuitively in the next chapter, but for now, know this: reading Tarot intuitively helps you to bring your energy and attention inward, discover your inner wisdom, and trust you have all the answers you need. The Tarot cards support this process by providing the imagery and symbolism you need to connect with your subconscious and intuitive mind, and ultimately, they reflect what you already know deep within.

There is no end to how you can use Tarot. It's all up to you and how it will best serve your Highest Good. There is no better time than right now to strengthen your connection with your intuition.

WHAT YOU CAN EXPECT
FROM THIS BOOK

Everywhere you look, there is a movement toward spirituality and conscious living. More and more people are turning to meditation, yoga, crystals, Reiki, and Tarot. Millennials are leading the charge for a more connected, fulfilled, conscious life. And Tarot meets those desires.

Step into any Urban Outfitters store and you'll find the *Wild Unknown Tarot* deck, Tarot-themed apparel, or an invitation to the latest Tarot Swap Meet.

You'll even find Tarot-inspired outfits from top designers like Christian Dior, and Tarot-inspired fragrances from Dolce & Gabbana.

Tarot has found its way into popular magazines such as *GOOP*, *Vogue*, *Teen Vogue*, and *Elle* and even into the business and news outlets at *Forbes*, *Entrepreneur*, *Wired*, and the *New York Times*.

In the past, Tarot was synonymous with crushed velvet, crystal balls, and Renaissance fairs. But now, Tarot is being seen in a new light—as the cutting-edge path to a deeper connection with the Higher Self.

We are truly waking up and becoming more aware of who we really are— soulful beings having a human experience in this lifetime. No longer will we plod through our days, accepting the status quo and allowing others to control us. No longer will we seek external validation; we want inner wisdom. Now it's about making conscious choices about who we want to be, what we want to create, and how we can manifest our fullest potential. And Tarot will help us get there. It gives us space and time to connect with our truest selves.

Tarot is no longer just a party trick to predict the future. It's a soulful tool to help you create the future you want by being your best self and using your inner wisdom and power to manifest your goals.

And that's what this book is about—offering a practical guide filled with actionable tips and exercises to help you unlock your inner wisdom and manifest your deepest desires. In these pages, you'll discover how anyone can use the Tarot to manifest their wildest dreams, create love-fueled relationships, set and achieve goals, fulfill your soul's purpose in work and life, make important decisions, and create the life you want. And you'll learn how to use your intuition to set goals, manifest those goals in alignment with your soul's purpose, and power up with the energy of the Tarot cards to achieve your dreams.

But let me be clear. This is not a "learn Tarot" book. I'll give you a quick crash course on how to read Tarot in chapter 2, but the best way to learn to read Tarot is to *read* Tarot. So even if you're a beginner worried that you don't know enough, just have a go. And if you would like to go deeper and build your Tarot skills, then check out my courses on www.biddytarot.com.

Now, beautiful soul-seeker, as you step into this journey of *Everyday Tarot*, I want to invite you to . . .

✳ **Make every day an intuitive, connected, and aligned experience in which you are looking at conscious choices about what you create.**

✳ **Open your mind, your heart, and your intuition—even just a bit. Even when it feels like it's getting too "woo-woo" or weird, just keep an open mind and give it a try.**

✳ **Be ready to go deeper into who you are—the good, the bad, and the ugly.**

✳   Trust that you have everything you need. All the answers lie within.

✳   Honor yourself and make time for you. Even just five minutes a day can impact your well-being.

✳   See Tarot as a part of your life, not just for "doing readings" but as something to integrate into your everyday being.

✳   Forget about doing it right. There is no "right" with Tarot. It's about trusting your intuition and doing it your way.

✳   Be ready to ask, *Who am I? And how can I live life to my fullest potential, in alignment with my Highest Good?*

───────────────◯───────────────

BONUS READER RESOURCES

I've created a reader resource kit just for you! It includes bonus worksheets, tutorials, tips, and resources to complement what I share in this book. To access your resources, visit www.everydaytarot.com/free.

And to learn more about Biddy Tarot, and me, visit www.biddytarot.com.

────────────────────────────────

This book is intended to make Tarot a living, breathing part of your life and it is a tool to take your practice to the next level. Dip in and out, or read it all at once. Play and experiment! The activities and techniques should get you started, but you can create your own or customize to your heart's content. You have my blessing!

As you're about to see, this ain't your grandma's Tarot!

CHAPTER 1

TAROT + INTUITION

SO, WHAT IS THE SIGNIFICANCE OF TAROT AND INTUITION?

If you are like me, you've got your Tarot cards in your hot little hands and can't wait to get straight into the juicy activities in this book. But hold up! Before we get into hands-on exercises, I want to take a moment to discuss what we're really doing here: accessing our inner wisdom and manifesting the future we most desire, using Tarot and intuition as our guide.

Learning how to use your Tarot cards is one thing. But understanding how to use them to connect with your intuition and your inner wisdom is another—*that* is the work we'll be doing here. Your inner wisdom is where the magic happens, where your true power shines through and you begin to create a whole new way of living inspired by your Highest Self and your soul purpose. It's time to tap into that.

WHAT IS INTUITION?

HAVE YOU EVER JUST KNOWN SOMETHING WITHOUT UNDERSTANDING HOW? That's your intuition at work. It gives you the ability to sense something innately and, in so doing, bridges the gap between the conscious and unconscious parts of your mind.

People typically experience intuition as an "inner knowing" or a gut feeling about something. I'll bet you can recall a time right now when you had a nagging feeling about something that you just couldn't shake. You couldn't explain why you felt that way, but it mattered to you.

For example, my friend Ineka had booked a romantic trip to Vietnam so she and her husband could take time out from their hectic family schedule for a week. But just after she locked in their plans, she started feeling that she needed to cancel the trip, even though it would mean losing the $500 deposit. Her husband wondered if she had gone crazy. She questioned herself too, but this intense notion was unshakable and Ineka knew she had to defy logic and cancel the booking.

She did, and thank goodness, because on the day they were meant to fly into Vietnam, a typhoon hit and the resort where they planned to stay was severely damaged. That's intuition—you can't explain why you feel the way you do, but you know it's real—even if others assume you've lost your mind.

Now, do you need to be gifted or special to access your intuition? No. I believe we are all intuitive—including you. It comes down to whether you *choose* to dial into your inner knowing or not. Think of intuition as radio waves; some people tune in automatically and have a perfect signal straightaway while others might need to work at it more to cut out the static.

Meditation, journaling, breathing, visualization, and, of course, reading Tarot cards are all things that will help you develop and tune in to your intuition. We'll explore these techniques as we go through the book.

HOW DOES INTUITION WORK?

While intuition can appear magical and mystical, it doesn't have to be.

Here's how intuition works. Your brain receives massive amounts of information every second. All that data is too much for the conscious mind to process at once, so lots of it gets pushed unprocessed into your subconscious for "storage." Your intuition absorbs this data in the subconscious mind, culls useful information, and then brings it into your awareness, so if you are paying attention, you can use it to take action.

Intuition is more than just a conduit for data, though. It helps you connect to your inner wisdom so that you don't have to rely on other people to tell you what to do. Your intuition helps you go deeper into who you are so that you can find flow and purpose in your life. It helps you manifest what you want by taking the path of least resistance toward your goal. Intuition enables you to let go of your ego and become more whole as you align with the Universe. I call it your superpower.

And Tarot? Well, Tarot is a tool to tap into your intuitive power and illuminate the wisdom of your Higher Self.

WHAT IS TAROT?

While many people expect that Tarot will tell you the future, predictions are not what Tarot cards are about. According to the Hermetic Order of the Golden Dawn, "The most powerful sources of information come from within; the Tarot aids in coming in contact with one's Higher Self."

Tarot is the storybook of our life, the mirror to our soul, and the key to our inner wisdom.

Every spiritual lesson we meet in our lives can be found in the seventy-eight Tarot cards. And when we consult the Tarot, we'll get shown the exact

lessons we need to learn and master to live an inspired life. It's like holding up a mirror to yourself so that you can access your subconscious mind and tap into the wisdom and answers that live in us all.

And there's no limit to what you can ask!

Many people turn to the Tarot cards to understand their relationships, career, finances, personal development, day-to-day situations, and major life transitions. You can use the Tarot to understand your past, your present, and your future. The cards won't tell you what will happen in specific detail—like the date when you'll meet your future husband—but they do give you insight into where you might be heading.

Best of all, the Tarot shows you how to make positive changes *now* so you can manifest your goals and your dreams.

You may already consciously know the message or insight you receive in a Tarot reading, in which case, the reading can be a heartening confirmation of what you were already thinking. On the other hand, you might be unaware of the message until you see it reflected in the cards.

It's as if the Tarot cards create an instant connection to our subconscious minds so we can access the inner wisdom of our Higher Self. From there we can bring it into our conscious awareness, where we can take action. Neat, right!?

Now, that doesn't quite explain what happens when you're reading for someone else and pick up that they're dating someone twenty years their junior and have told no one about it (true story!). What's that all about?

Well, here is where things might be a little more "out there" and magical. You see, we are all linked to a collective, universal wisdom in addition to our inner wisdom. And when we read the Tarot cards—and connect with our intuition—we can tap into this universal wisdom as well. Just imagine what might be possible for you with limitless, timeless knowledge at your fingertips!

This is why reading the Tarot cards intuitively can be so powerful, particularly when you do it for yourself. Learning book meanings is one thing, but when you find out how to read the cards intuitively, you get an instant connection with your inner wisdom—I'll show you how in chapter 2. And when you read Tarot for yourself, you can see, hear, and feel the messages that are for you and no one else. The energy is so much more powerful. Instead of relying on someone else, you learn to rely on your inner wisdom.

For example, let's say you pull the Nine of Pentacles for your daily card. You could look this up in a book and discover that it means self-reliance, independence, and wealth. But when you tune in to the card, your eyes are drawn to the little snail sliding his way through a beautiful garden. It reminds you to slow down and enjoy the ride.

HERE'S WHAT HAPPENS WHEN YOU READ TAROT AND ACCESS YOUR INTUITION

✳   You have an inner guidance system available to you.

✳   You learn more about yourself.

✳   You become more conscious.

✳   You make better decisions.

✳   You reclaim your power and free will.

✳   You learn more about life and humanity.

✳   You can support others to discover themselves.

✳   You have better relationships.

Many people think that Tarot is nothing more than drawing a card and getting an answer. But to me, Tarot's message is more powerful when you interpret a card alongside your intuition and what you know about your situation.

In fact, I recommend you start by checking in with yourself first while drawing on multiple sources of information—intuition, data, other people's ideas, etc. Then, consult the Tarot cards to take you deeper into your subconscious mind and see what might not be on top in your conscious mind. Tarot reading gives you that next layer on what you already know *and* teaches you to trust your inner wisdom, rather than relying on an external source to give you the answers.

Tarot is perfect for self-development, making choices, manifesting goals, coaching others, planning a business, writing a book, meditating—you name it. There's no limit to how you can use it.

I hope by now that you're even more fired up to integrate Tarot into your everyday life. But just in case you're still holding back, I will tackle a few roadblocks that might sit in your way.

BUSTING THE MYTHS ABOUT TAROT

There are more myths about Tarot than about ancient deities!

Ask the average person on the street what they know about Tarot, and you might hear things like:

"Tarot tells you the future!"

"I'm too scared to get a Tarot reading. What if something bad happens?!"

"Tarot is the work of the devil!"

Sadly, Tarot seems to be one of the most misunderstood spiritual tools out there. And yet, it has the power to help so many people on a deeply personal and soulful level.

So let's do some serious myth-busting, shall we?

MYTH 1

YOU HAVE TO BE PSYCHIC TO READ TAROT

· ✳ · ·

Many people will have you believe that you have to be psychic to read Tarot.

They think you have to have some supernatural power that allows you to see into the future, know what people are thinking, or receive messages from the Spirit World to be a good Tarot reader.

They're wrong. You don't have to be psychic to be a good Tarot reader. In fact, anyone can learn to read Tarot—including you.

Many people have shut down their intuition by refusing to listen to their inner voice, passing it off as a silly feeling that means nothing. They opt for concepts that can be explained by science and fact-based research.

Those who say "no" to their intuition close themselves off to their fullest potential.

I hope you'll say "yes" instead.

Say yes to those intuitive feelings you have about the people you love and their well-being. Say yes to those random, unexplainable messages you might receive that help you navigate your life's path. And say yes to going with your heart and not just your head.

When you do, you open yourself to so many of life's possibilities.

MYTH 2

TAROT IS EVIL AND MAKES BAD THINGS HAPPEN

· ✳ · ·

You've seen it in the movies: the Tarot reader pulls the Death card from the deck, and suddenly her client crashes to the floor, stone dead!

Sadly, it's scenes like these that have made people fear that if they consult the Tarot cards, something terrible might happen. They might die. Their relationship might end. They might lose their job. They might have an accident. And so on.

But do you believe that a small card with a picture on it can kill someone? Really?

The Tarot doesn't *make* something happen, good or bad. It doesn't make you do anything. (Thank you, free will!) Tarot is merely a tool that gives you guidance to help you make better decisions and take the right actions to achieve your goals.

Whether Tarot is evil and the work of the devil . . . well, I won't argue with any deeply ingrained spiritual beliefs. But there's one thing I know for sure: Tarot has this beautiful way of connecting you to your inner wisdom, your inner sanctuary, and your soul. And I believe that is where God lives.

MYTH 3
TAROT TELLS YOU THE FUTURE

· ✴ ✦ ✴ ·

One of the biggest myths about Tarot is that it shows you the future:

Want to know when you'll get married? Ask the Tarot!

Want to know if you'll get your dream job? Pull out those Tarot cards!

At least, that's what many people *think* you can do with the Tarot cards.

Here's the thing: while you can use the Tarot cards to predict what *might* happen, is that where you want to focus your attention and energy?

Think about it. If the Tarot cards said, "Awesome! That dream job you've always wanted is coming to you in August!" how might that impact what you do next? Would you still work as hard, knowing that the job was yours? Or would you relax? And if you relaxed, would you still get the job, or would your actions change the outcome?

What if you don't get the answer you want? What if the Tarot cards said, "Hey, sorry, but there's no wedding on the horizon"? Would you just give up on your dream to get married? Or would you shop around for a Tarot reader who would give you the answer you want?

When you ask about the future, you're assuming it's all laid out in front of you and there's little you can do to change it. That's great if you get the answer you want, but you'll be left feeling powerless and deflated if you get bad news.

No. The best way to predict your future is to *create* it.

While the Tarot cards can give you insight into what might be around the corner, they are much more powerful when you use them to understand the present. When you understand the current influences in your life, you're in a much stronger position to shape your future.

If you want to find out when you'll get married, focus on what actions you can take now to meet the partner of your dreams and create a fulfilling, long-lasting relationship. And if you want to find out if you'll get your dream job, focus on the opportunities available to you right now, so that you can manifest it down the road.

Wouldn't you prefer to feel empowered by the Tarot cards and your intuition than to be told what might or might not happen?

When it comes to Tarot, fortune-telling is *out*, and intuition is *in*—especially if you want to create your best future and manifest your goals.

Now, there's one more myth that I want to bust—and it's one that I get asked all the time.

MYTH 4
AM I WEIRD FOR READING TAROT?

Listen to me right now: you are not "weird" for reading Tarot. All different types of people consult the Tarot cards—lawyers, teachers, management consultants, artists, stay-at-home parents, mystics, musicians—you name it. You're only weird if you think you're weird. I used to feel a bit funny about telling other people I read Tarot. But one evening after two glasses of wine at a corporate networking event, I mentioned that I read Tarot cards to a fifty-something-year-old man in a suit. I presumed he'd make a quick exit. Instead he lit up with excitement and said, "Oh! Me too! What's your favorite deck?"

Tarot is available to anyone who wants to understand herself better and live a fulfilling, purposeful life—including you! Be it a trickle of good juju or a full spiritual awakening, just be open to whatever experience you have.

You know, I always find it interesting when someone expresses concern that others will think she's weird for reading Tarot. It is a crystal clear illustration of the clash between intuition and ego: "I feel drawn to Tarot . . . but I'm worried about what others might think." Can you tell which side is which? And if so, which voice would you rather listen to?

EGO VS. INTUITION AND HOW TO TELL THE DIFFERENCE

Many people struggle to know when to trust their intuition. But the question isn't, "Can I trust my intuition?" Instead, it's often, "Is this my intuition or my ego?"

Intuition comes from a place of love and abundance where everything serves your Higher Self and even the challenging periods in your life will benefit you. Your intuition gives you what you need, not just what you think you want. On the other hand, ego comes from a place of fear and lack. Your ego worries that you will miss out on something or lose something. Your ego might tempt you with what you *want*, but as you discover later, it's not what you need. So are the thoughts or sensations bubbling up sending you messages of abundance or lack? Fear or love?

You can also discern your intuition's messages from those of your ego by observing where they are coming from within your body. Intuition often manifests as a sensation in the heart or stomach (that's why it's called a "gut feeling"!). Ego speaks through the head (it's why we say, "I'm so in my head right now"). When you want to access your intuition, bring your awareness into your heart or stomach—specifically, your solar plexus—and feel from there instead of thinking from your head.

Finally, intuition often expresses itself as a persistent "inner voice" that gets louder and louder over an extended period. Ego may *sound* like an inner voice, but it acts more like a two-year-old, demanding your attention *right now*, before being attracted to the next shiny object and taking your notice there.

So now that you know how to recognize the voice of your intuition, I want to show you what's possible when you answer the call of your Higher Self—even when that sounds like a wacky idea.

TAROT *AND* INTUITION IN ACTION

In 2016, my husband Anthony and I were getting restless. Our two daughters were five and seven years old and needed their own bedrooms. We were also feeling a pull away from the city life we had grown up with, to somewhere with more nature and space. We knew we needed to get out of our three-bedroom town house with a tiny courtyard and into something more spacious in a natural setting.

We started to look at places within a ninety-minute drive from Melbourne, because both our families lived nearby and we knew they wanted to see their grandchildren grow up. Although we had spent a good six months looking for properties, we didn't feel we were on the right path. My husband and I both had been keen on one place and had organized for my father-in-law to bid at the auction while we were on holiday in the Philippines. But it just wasn't meant to be, and the house sold way above the asking price.

It was frustrating; both of us wanted a change so much, but we kept hitting roadblocks. I wondered, "Is it just not meant to be? Is our intuition leading us astray?" (Hello, ego and fear!) I pulled a Tarot card—the Nine of Wands. If we wanted to do this, we needed to push forward. And with a Nine—well, we were supposedly near the finish line, even if we didn't realize it.

So, we explored the possibility of moving further afield, up north where the weather is warm and the landscape is lush. We dreamed about the beautiful places where people spend their holidays and wondered how it might be to live there.

To see if it was, indeed, what we wanted, we traveled up to Queensland and northern New South Wales in September 2016 and spent a week each in three different areas: the Sunshine Coast, Gold Coast, and Byron Bay. The Gold Coast was too busy for us. Byron Bay was too expensive. But the Sunshine Coast was just right. While we were there, we went to over fifteen house inspections on the off-chance we might find our dream home then and there. While we didn't come across a perfect match, we were 100 percent sure we wanted to move to the Sunshine Coast.

Once we returned home, my brain went into overdrive. You see, when I want something, I get to work to manifest it as soon as possible. So I was busy planning and plotting how we could buy a house in our new target area as fast as we could. But I could feel myself getting frustrated again (welcome back, ego). We had two kids, and a plane trip there and back was around $400 per person. Going up to the Sunshine Coast every weekend to inspect houses as a family just wouldn't be possible. How on earth were we going to find our dream home when we were stuck in Melbourne, a two-and-a-half-hour plane ride away?

My brain kept trying to figure things out, and I even mulled over whether we ought to just buy one of the houses we had seen in September. I mean, a few of them were fine—but they weren't great. The best were still an eight out of ten, instead of a ten out of ten. But surely we could settle for an "eight" house and avoid the extra time and travel of trying to find a "ten"?

While my brain was working out how to find a house, my intuition began creeping in. I had a strong sense that we would know when we had found the right house, but it wouldn't be straightaway. My gut feeling was that we would find the house in late November and move in in February. And in my Tarot readings, I kept pulling the Ten of Cups (a family celebrating an idyllic new home). Despite the positive signs, my brain and my ego kept questioning whether it was possible to buy a house and move in just two months. It defied logic. But we'd give it a go and see what came our way.

We looked at our calendars and saw that we had one weekend free at the end of November where we could leave the kids with my mum and head to the Sunshine Coast for a whirlwind thirty-six-hour trip. Anthony called the real estate agents and lined up about nine properties for us to visit. And I was super-excited because everything was fitting in with my intuitive insights about finding a place in late November.

But by the ninth house, we had still only found more "eight" houses and not the dreamy "ten" I had envisioned. We had gone to get a coffee and chat about the places we had seen when Anthony pulled out his phone and saw a new alert. One of the dream places we had on our list had dropped by $100,000. The only problem was that it was still $100,000 above our budget. We chose to go and see it anyway. I warned Anthony, "You realize that we're about to walk into this place and fall in love straightaway? Are you ready for that?" And it was true.

As soon as I walked through into the wide-open space inside, I lost my heart to the house. This place had everything we wanted: a beautiful, modern interior; huge windows so that it felt as though you were living inside while still enjoying the fresh air; a huge pool, with a Bali-inspired outbuilding surrounded by luscious gardens; a veggie patch, a private forest, a "fairy lake," and even a creek and rock face. I'm not kidding—everything I had ever dreamed of in a home was *all* on this property.

And then I saw the Starchild Tarot deck in one of the rooms. It was a divine sign!

I turned to Anthony and said, "Get the contract. We're buying this place."

Once we had emerged from our ecstatic state, we put together a plan for how we might afford this over-budget home (welcome back, fear-based ego). Our Melbourne home was nearly paid off, but this new home would require us to start another mortgage—something I didn't want to do. Anthony calculated it would take another five to ten years to pay it off, but we were ready to do it.

We set the auction date for our old home February 4, with the settlement of the new home on February 9. It lined up wonderfully with my gut feeling that we'd move in February.

Our Melbourne home sold for a staggering $200,000 above the auction reserve price, which meant we didn't need as big a mortgage as we thought. Plus, the business did exceptionally well in 2017. So in just nine months, we had paid off the new mortgage. The Universe had taken care of us.

The moral of this story? You know more than you realize. Trust your intuition, and it will take you to the most beautiful places. Even if your mind thinks it's not possible, it totally is—sometimes you just need a little extra clarity or reassurance. And that's where Tarot comes in.

HOW TO LEARN TAROT

In the next chapter, we will dive into the fundamentals of reading Tarot.

Learning to read Tarot is more about finding out how to access your intuition than understanding the techniques. Some would have you believe that you must study years and years to master Tarot. However, I think that you can read Tarot straightaway if you are ready to say yes to your intuition and keep an open mind. As Bakara Wintner (author of *WTF is Tarot*) says, "You do not need to learn Tarot—you already know it." You have everything you need inside of you, and the Tarot cards will help you access it.

In chapter 2, I give you a crash course in how to read the Tarot cards. It's designed to get you started so that you can do the activities in this book without having read Tarot cards before. Will you need more support? Possibly. It depends on how you prefer to learn. If you do, go to www.biddytarot.com and take one of our online courses on Tarot.

Here are a few quick tips on how to get the most out of your Tarot cards:

1. Know that you can read the cards now—even if you're a total beginner.

2. Know that you do not need special gifts or knowledge to understand the Tarot. You only need to say yes to your intuition and trust your inner wisdom.

3. Connect your personal experiences to the cards. The more you can personalize what the cards mean to you, the better your reading will be. How do your experiences and life lessons relate to each card? Your life brings the Tarot cards to life.

4. Be around people who support you and who can respect your journey toward being the best version of yourself.

5. Know that inner guidance is always available to you.

The best way to learn Tarot is *not* to read more books about Tarot (except this one!). Read books about life, spirituality, personal development, relationships—anything that helps you understand the human experience will bring so much more depth to your readings and your intuitive insights.

Once you start to open yourself to the potential that Tarot offers, you'll see that so much exists within these little pieces of cardboard.

Instead of looking for answers outside of yourself, trusting others to show you the way, you will reclaim your power and honor the sacred insight you have within. You are about to go deep and reconnect with your intuition and your inner guidance. Tarot is merely the tool or the vehicle to help you do that.

CHAPTER 2
A QUICK-START GUIDE TO TAROT

BEFORE WE DIVE INTO HOW YOU CAN USE TAROT IN YOUR EVERYDAY life, I want to give you my quick-start guide to the Tarot cards. I'll show you what Tarot *really* is, how to interpret the Tarot cards, and how to perform Tarot readings with confidence.

If you're a total beginner, this chapter will give you the self-assurance you need to read the cards intuitively. And if you have a little more experience under your belt, this chapter might just be the refresher you need to see things from an entirely new perspective.

Now, is this chapter going to give you everything you need to know about Tarot? No. That comes through daily practice, deep learning, and self-exploration. Tarot is a lifelong journey where you never truly master the cards; there's always something new popping up.

WANT TO LEARN MORE ABOUT TAROT?

If you feel called to take your Tarot skills and knowledge further than what I share in this book, then check out my courses at www.biddytarot.com/shop.

HOW TO CHOOSE YOUR
FIRST TAROT DECK

If you want to read Tarot, first you need a deck.

The most popular Tarot deck is the Rider-Waite deck, and my favorite version is the Radiant Rider-Waite. Most books, websites, and learning resources reference this deck, so it's perfect for the Tarot beginner. Each card tells a clear story and contains rich, traditional symbolism which aids in intuitively connecting with the deeper spiritual message of the cards.

However, the Rider-Waite deck doesn't speak to everyone. The imagery is more classical—think kings, capes, and castles—and it is widely used by all kinds of Tarot readers. So if you're a modern mystic, this deck might not gel with you. Luckily, there are thousands of other Tarot decks you can choose from in that case, from more traditional decks—such as the Tarot de Marseille, Thoth Tarot, and the Visconti Tarot—to modern ones—such as Everyday Tarot, Lumina, and Wild Unknown. Heck, there's even a Hello Kitty deck and a *Game of Thrones* deck!

To find a deck that's right for you, jump online and browse through Pinterest, Instagram, and Google to find the cards that are appealing to you. If you have a local New Age store, that's even better—you can check out your options and get a feel for which is the right fit for you.

When it comes time to choose your Tarot deck, consider the following questions:

✴ **Do you like the look of the deck? Are you intuitively connecting to it?**

✴ **Can you read the pictures, or do you need more information to interpret the cards?**

✴ **What other resources are available to learn more about the card meanings for the deck?**

★ Does this deck match your experience level? Simple decks are great for beginners, and more complex ones work for pros.

★ Is the actual card of good quality? There's no point buying a gorgeous deck only to find it falls apart within months!

Finally, there's a rumor going around that Tarot cards should only ever be given to you and you can't buy your own. That's baloney! Of course, you can buy your own Tarot deck—and I recommend that you do. That way you'll find a deck that connects with *you,* rather than what someone else thinks you might like.

TAROT VS. ORACLE DECKS

As you're choosing your first deck, be sure to choose a Tarot deck rather than an Oracle deck.

What's the difference? Tarot decks all have a similar structure: seventy-eight cards with twenty-two Major Arcana cards and fifty-six Minor Arcana cards. Although the visual elements vary between Tarot decks, there is typically a core essence to each card that you see across all decks.

Oracle decks are more free-flowing. There is no set number of cards, structures, or common meanings. Oracle decks draw from multiple sources of inspiration—angels, goddesses, positive affirmations, poets, and so on.

In a reading, I find that Oracle cards highlight the core themes or energies present, whereas the Tarot cards give more detail about what's happening and why.

Tarot and Oracle cards can work together in beautiful ways, but for this guide, we'll be focusing only on the Tarot, so make sure you choose a *Tarot* deck!

GETTING TO KNOW YOUR TAROT CARDS

You've bought your Tarot deck, so now it's time to get to know your Tarot cards and discover what they mean!

A word of caution: learning the Tarot card meanings is a lifelong journey, and it would be impossible to teach you every card in just a few pages. My intention here is to give you what you need to get started and encourage you to continue your discovery from there.

For now, let's get you up to speed on the basics!

FAMILIARIZE YOURSELF WITH THE TAROT CARDS

The first thing you want to do when you get your new Tarot deck is to familiarize yourself with all seventy-eight Tarot cards.

Take out your deck and go through it, card by card, looking at the imagery and repeating the name of each card. The goal is to get a general feel for the deck and connect with its overall energy.

Then go through the deck again, but this time, spend at least a few minutes with each card. As you look at each one, pay attention to the details of the image.

As you go through your deck several times, you might start to notice a particular "energy" to each card. You might get a feeling, a sensation, a thought, or even a phrase that comes to mind. This is beautiful—it's your intuition shining through and showing you what this card might mean! So pay attention and note what comes to you. Resist the temptation at this point to look up the card's meaning right away to see if you got it "right"! Your intuitive feel for the card is most important.

Repeat this process until you can select a card at random and recognize it immediately.

LEARN THE BASIC MEANINGS OF THE CARDS

Now that you're familiar with your Tarot deck, it's time to learn about the basic structure of the deck and the meanings of the cards.

The deck is separated into twenty-two Major Arcana cards and fifty-six Minor Arcana cards (including the Court Cards). The Minor Arcana comprises four Suits—Cups, Pentacles, Swords, and Wands. Within each Suit, there are ten numbered cards from the Ace to the Ten and four Court Cards.

THE MAJOR ARCANA

The Major Arcana includes twenty-one numbered cards and one unnumbered card (the Fool). These cards represent life lessons, karmic influences, and the big archetypal themes that are influencing your life and your soul's journey to enlightenment.

The Major Arcana cards are deep and complex in beautiful ways! These cards symbolize the structure of human consciousness and hold the keys to life lessons passed down through the ages.

When you see a Major Arcana card in a Tarot reading, you are being called to reflect on the lessons and themes that have appeared in your path.

When a Tarot reading is mostly Major Arcana cards, you are experiencing life-changing events that will have long-term effects. There are valuable lessons that you must pay attention to if you want to progress further in your spiritual and personal quest.

THE MINOR ARCANA

While the Major Arcana reveal events that will occur due to laws of the Universe, the Minor Arcana show events that occur due to laws of human nature. Therefore, the Minor Arcana highlight the more practical aspects of life and can refer to current issues that will have a temporary or minor influence.

In a Tarot reading, a Minor Arcana card will tell you about a specific situation or event that's happening in your life. It's a situation that is temporary and has the potential to change into something different. If the Minor Arcana

Tarot cards are predominant in your reading, you are dealing with day-to-day issues that will not have a lasting influence on your life. These matters are passing through, presenting you with an opportunity to learn from them. (Look to any Major Arcana cards to understand how they may impact your life in the long term.)

The Suits

The Minor Arcana is split into the four Suits of Cups, Pentacles, Swords, and Wands, with each corresponding to one of the four metaphysical elements.

BASIC MEANINGS OF THE SUITS		
SUIT	ELEMENT	MEANING
Cups	Water	Emotions, relationships, feelings, and creativity
Pentacles	Earth	Money, financial resources, material possessions, career, and the physical realm
Swords	Air	Power, rationality, the intellect, and thoughts
Wands	Fire	Inspiration, spirituality, ideas, and energy flow

The Numbered Cards

Within each Suit, there are ten numbered cards, from Ace to Ten. To understand the forty numbered cards in the Minor Arcana, combine the energy of the Suit with that of the Number. For example, the Five of Pentacles relates to change or conflict (fives) in financial matters (Pentacles).

THE BASIC MEANINGS OF THE NUMBERS

1
New beginning

6
Harmony and growth

2
Partnership

7
Attainment and understanding

3
Creation

8
Mastery and power

4
Stability and foundations

9
Fruition and fulfillment

5
Conflict and change

10
Completion and ending

The Court Cards

The Court Cards are the four "royal" cards—the Page, Knight, Queen, and King—within each Suit, for a total of sixteen cards.

Court Cards typically relate to aspects of your personality that are being expressed in a particular situation. For example, the Queen of Wands is a warm, friendly, and sociable person. If she shows in a career reading, you are bringing these qualities to your work situation.

The Court Cards blend the characteristics of the Page, Knight, Queen, or King with those of the assigned Suit.

THE BASIC MEANINGS OF THE COURTS

PAGES
Ready to explore a new opportunity or project

KNIGHTS
In pursuit of a mission, action-oriented

QUEENS
Mature, receptive, and leads from a place of inner power

KINGS
Mature, dominant, authoritative, and leads from

a place of outer power

HOW TO INTUITIVELY READ
A TAROT CARD

Many Tarot beginners believe that they need to memorize all seventy-eight Tarot cards to be a good Tarot reader. But this is the wrong way to go about it! Why? It's boring. It takes forever. And it doesn't work. Rote learning will render your readings robotic and lifeless.

It's better to learn how to intuitively interpret the Tarot cards so that you can read any card without having to rely on memorized meanings.

But it's useful to talk about the difference between those traditional Tarot card meanings people often memorize and intuitive Tarot card meanings.

TRADITIONAL VS. INTUITIVE TAROT CARD MEANINGS

· ✳ ✷ ✳ ·

There are two ways of interpreting the Tarot cards:

(1) **From the book with traditional meanings**

(2) **From the heart with intuitive meanings**

Traditional card meanings do serve a purpose. They connect us to the collective wisdom and history of the Tarot and provide the backbone of what the Tarot cards refer to. You'll find them in Tarot books and websites like my own (www.biddytarot.com), and they often link to deeper symbolic and esoteric systems.

Intuitive card meanings serve a different purpose. They connect you to your own inner wisdom, creating a sense for the card that won't exist in a book but is profound to *you*. For example, you might see the Moon card in a reading about reaching a goal, and be reminded of the phrase, "Shoot for the moon." You see it as a sign that you'll achieve your goal, and that turns out to be right . . . but you won't find this meaning in a book.

With enough practice, you'll be able to tap into both the traditional and intuitive meanings in a Tarot reading, knowing when to use one or the other. Don't rely on just one method!

HOW TO INTUITIVELY INTERPRET A TAROT CARD

Intuitively interpreting a Tarot card is all about tuning in to your inner wisdom, your heart, your feelings, your emotions, and your energy about the card.

Start by clearing your mind and grounding your energy. This can be as simple as taking two deep, slow breaths or meditating for five minutes.

The more that you can create space around you and let your mind relax, the more you will connect with the intuitive messages.

Next, pose a question for the cards. For example, "What energy do I need to know about today?"

Shuffle the cards, and when you feel ready, draw one from the top of the deck.

First, gaze at the card and take in its imagery. You don't need to interpret it; just allow the imagery to sink into your mind, moving from your conscious to subconscious, which is where your intuition lives.

Notice your energy as you look at the card. How does it make you feel? Do you feel excited? Happy? Sad?

Do you have any physical sensations when you look at this card? Where is it and how does that feel?

And do any thoughts, words, images, or phrases come to mind as you look at the card?

Pay attention to any or all of these subtle messages that come to you.

Now, describe what you see in the card and tell the story of what's happening. Who is in the picture and what are they doing? What objects do you see? What is the landscape like? Are there any symbols that you recognize?

As you describe the card, you might also find your eye drawn to a smaller detail on the card. This is often your intuition talking to you and showing you what you need to see.

Finally, take everything you have experienced with the card so far and ask, "How does this relate to my life right now?" Often you'll see a metaphor for something happening with you.

For example, the Eight of Pentacles shows a man working diligently on creating beautiful coins. You might ask yourself, "What am I working on diligently right now? And why is it important?"

You might also follow your curiosity and read more about this card in a book to discover its traditional meaning. That is fine. Just be mindful of doing this *after* you intuitively interpret the card and see it as *additional* information rather than validation about whether you got it "right."

HOW TO DO A THREE-CARD REACTION FOR YOURSELF

By now, you're familiar with what the cards mean and how to interpret a card intuitively. It's time to bring these skills together and do a three-card reading.

If you're an absolute beginner, you might start to freak out and think, "But Brigit, I can't do a Tarot reading yet! I've only just started!" Never fear, my dear. You are even more prepared than you realize. In fact, you were ready the moment you thought about the Tarot for the first time. Now it's just a matter of making that thought a reality.

When you begin to do your own Tarot readings, a beautiful thing happens. You see how the Tarot cards come alive. You feel a strengthening connection to your inner wisdom and intuition, and you notice how the Tarot cards support you in opening up this relationship. The earlier you start, the sooner you can make these beautiful, intuitive connections.

It's a cycle. The more you read with the cards, the more you learn. And the more you learn, the more you can read with the cards.

So, start now. Let's go!

STEP 1:
CLEAR YOUR MIND

· * ✳ * ·

You might think a Tarot reading starts when you pick up the cards and shuffle them. But a Tarot reading begins from the moment you decide now is the time to consult the cards.

To create the most intuitive, clear readings for yourself, you need to begin with a clear mind. Here are two (of many) ways you can make that happen:

(1) **TAKE THREE DEEP BREATHS. On the first exhalation, relax. On the second exhalation, be present. And on the third exhalation, open your mind to receive.**

(2) **MEDITATE. Close your eyes. Pay attention to your breath, feeling the warm air in your nostrils. Observe any thoughts that come to your mind, and watch them float away like clouds. Spend another minute in this place of peace before opening your eyes.**

Beautiful. You're now ready to begin your reading.

STEP 2:
ASK A QUESTION

With a clear mind, ask yourself what you need to know right now.

For example, you're worried about a lack of connection in your relationship with your partner. So you ask, "What do I need to know about my relationship right now?" or "How can I create more connection between myself and my partner?"

Or you might wonder if you'll get the promotion you've been dreaming about. So you ask, "What can I do to increase my chances of getting the promotion?" or "What is the energy surrounding this situation?"

Notice how I haven't asked, "Will I get the job?" or "Will my relationship improve?" When you ask these kinds of questions, you're assuming your future is set in stone and there's little you can do to change it.

Similarly, if you ask, "Should I go for the promotion?" you assume that the Tarot cards will make your decision for you. No, you have free will and it is up to *you* to decide.

MY FAVORITE QUESTIONS TO ASK THE TAROT

To help you stay in this beautiful place of curiosity, empowerment, and manifestation, here are some of my favorite questions to ask the cards:

✳ What do I need to know about this situation?

✳ What is the energy surrounding this situation?

✳ How can I achieve my desired outcome?

Over time, you'll find your favorites too.

Once you have your question, write it down, so it's clear in your mind.

STEP 3:
SHUFFLE AND LAY OUT THE CARDS
· ✳ ✳ ·

Now you're ready to pick up your cards and shuffle. As you do, channel your energy into the reading and focus on your question.

Then, when you feel ready, lay out the three cards for your reading. Lay them side by side, from left to right, faceup.

STEP 4:
READ THE CARDS AND ANSWER YOUR QUESTION

· ✳ ✦ ✳ ·

This is the fun part! Go through each card, from left to right, and interpret what it means for you. Use the techniques you learned with single cards to read each card intuitively, writing your insights as you go. And if you need a little extra support, consult your favorite Tarot guide to discover the traditional meaning of the card. Remember, though, only look at the book after you have explored the card intuitively.

Once you have interpreted each card, look at the whole spread, as if it were a three-page storybook. What's the story the cards are telling you?

Now go back to your original question and answer it based on what you have explored within the cards.

Write the complete reading in your notebook, including the question you asked, the cards, your interpretations, and your answer. Come back to these insights later to reflect and learn from what transpired after the reading.

And, voilà, you're done!

HOW TO TELL THE STORY
IN AN ENTIRE READING

Whether you're using a three-card spread or a ten-card spread, it's possible to create meaningful connections and tell the story in an entire reading.

Here's how:

1. **TELL THE STORY IN EACH CARD.**

2. Look for **MEANINGFUL COMBINATIONS** and tell the combined story.

3. Look for **KEY THEMES AND PATTERNS** across all the cards in the reading.

4. **PAY ATTENTION TO THE BALANCE** of Minor and Major Arcana cards, Suits, and Numbers.

5. **LOOK FOR THE MAJOR ARCANA CARDS.** What is the story connecting these cards? And how do the Minor Arcana cards support this story?

6. Bring together what you have discovered and **WRITE THE STORY** of the reading.

Remember to start small. Begin by telling the story across a three-card reading. As your confidence grows, so can the size of your spreads. Soon you'll be able to read the story within a more complex spread like the ten-card Celtic Cross!

HELP!

Do you need help with your reading? Here are a few common situations that come up when people read the cards for themselves and what to do about them.

MY READING MAKES LITTLE SENSE!

· ✳ ✴ ✳ ·

Sometimes you may find that there are messages in the cards that make little sense. It doesn't mean the reading is wrong. It may just be a sign that you're not ready for the message yet.

Note down your insights, even if you don't understand them. Then come back to your reading in a week or a month to see if it takes on new strength for you. Sometimes events need to unfold further before a reading resonates.

IT'S NOT WHAT I WANT TO HEAR

· ✳ ✴ ✳ ·

Sometimes you may receive a message that is challenging to hear. For example, the cards may show that there are deep-seated issues in what you thought was a dreamy relationship.

Go back to why you asked about your relationship. Perhaps your subconscious mind knew something was up, but it's taking your conscious mind a little longer to catch up.

Get curious and open up to exploring whatever comes up in a reading, even the darker shadows. If the cards are showing you something you haven't realized yet, be ready to go deeper and ask what it's all about. Draw more Tarot cards if you need a little more support.

AM I JUST MAKING THIS UP?

· ✳ ✴ ✳ ·

Sometimes you may receive a positive message and wonder if you're just making it up or if it's your intuition doing the talking. (It's funny how we can't always embrace our own success!)

If you do the work up front to clear your mind and connect with your Higher Self, then your reading will reflect your intuition, rather than your ego. You need to trust yourself and trust that the message is from your Higher Self.

THREE SIMPLE AND EASY TAROT SPREADS

Sure, there are tons of complicated Tarot spreads that have ten, twenty, even all seventy-eight Tarot cards in them. But if you want to get to the heart of the matter, then I recommend you start with a simple three-card Tarot reading. Seriously, you can get super-deep with just three cards.

Here are three of my favorite three-card Tarot spreads for you to use in your readings.

1) PAST-PRESENT-FUTURE SPREAD

· ✳ ✴ ✳ ·

The Past-Present-Future Spread is one of the most popular Tarot spreads because it is so insightful and straightforward.

It works well for both general and specific situations where you want to understand the timeline of events related to that situation. Let's break it down:

✴   **The Past shows you what has led you to where you are now.**

✴   **The Present shows you where you are now.**

✳ **The Future shows you where you are heading, based on where you are now.**

Can you see a pattern here? While the spread is called "Past-Present-Future," it's all in the "here and now" because that is where you can take action!

EXAMPLE READING

QUESTION: *What do I need to know about my career?*

PAST: *Eight of Wands.* You have had a swift progression through your career. You may have had to frequently travel by air as a part of your job.

PRESENT: *Four of Cups.* You are at a point where that fast-paced work life no longer suits you and you are saying no to these opportunities now.

FUTURE: *Ten of Cups.* You envision a future where you can spend more time with your family at home. Travel is no longer an option. Work may become less of a priority to you, with family being your ultimate focus.

ANSWER: You're going through a transition in your career, where regular travel and a fast-paced work life no longer meet your needs. You are establishing new boundaries in your career so you can prioritize your family instead.

2) SITUATION-PROBLEM-ADVICE SPREAD

· ✴ ✦ ✴ · ·

The Situation-Problem-Advice Spread is one of my favorites because it's all about creating the outcomes you most desire. Use this spread for both general and specific situations to gain insight into what you need to do to get a situation back on track and heading in the right direction.

Let's break it down:

✴   Situation—What you are experiencing right now

✴   Problem—The core issue or challenge that you're facing

✴   Advice—What action you can take to achieve your goals

EXAMPLE READING

QUESTION: *How can I trust my intuition more?*

EIGHT OF PENTACLES   KNIGHT OF SWORDS   THE HANGED MAN

SITUATION: *Eight of Pentacles.* You are working hard to become more intuitive, taking lessons and doing repetitive activities to improve.

PROBLEM: *Knight of Swords.* The core issue is that you are striving to be more intuitive through repeated action and pushing forward.

ADVICE: *Hanged Man.* At the heart of it, you need to surrender to your intuition and look at this from a new perspective. Intuition is not about *doing* but about *being.*

ANSWER: Instead of trying so hard to be more intuitive, surrender to the process and allow your intuition to be a part of your life.

3) THE "NO SPREAD" SPREAD

· * ✳ * ·

The "No Spread" Spread is a fun, flexible, and dynamic spread perfect for all kinds of readings. It's called the "No Spread" Spread because it has no predetermined spread positions. Instead, the previous card determines the positions.

Draw the first card, interpret it, and then create the next position from that card. Let me show you how.

EXAMPLE READING

QUESTION: What do I need to know about my new romantic relationship?

Shuffle the cards and spread them out into a fan shape, so you can select cards from the fan as you go.

PAGE OF CUPS

FIRST CARD: *Page of Cups.* You are exploring new emotions and feelings in a way that you haven't experienced before. You are in a phase of discovery and curiosity.

After you interpret the first card, what new question comes up? Here, the Page of Cups might lead you to ask, "What am I learning as part of this relationship?"

QUEEN OF WANDS

SECOND CARD (What am I learning as part of this relationship?): *Queen of Wands.* You're learning to become more expressive, compassionate, social, and energized. Your heart is opening, and you welcome this person into your life.

Now, what new question comes up? Here, the Queen of Wands might lead you to ask, "How can I take this expressive and compassionate energy and create a positive relationship?"

TWO OF CUPS

THIRD CARD (How can I take this expressive and compassionate energy and create a positive relationship?): *Two of Cups.* You can create a deeper connection with each other by seeing the good in one another. If you are embodying the Queen of Wands, how can you see the Queen of Wands in him also?

Continue to ask further questions based on the cards drawn until you feel the reading seems complete and you have the insight you need.

HOW TO READ TAROT WITH CONFIDENCE

Congratulations! By now, you know how to interpret the cards intuitively, do a simple three-card reading, and tell the story in the cards.

This is just the beginning, but I have a good feeling your connection with your Tarot cards and your intuition will just grow and grow. In the meantime, here is what I wish I had known when I was learning to read Tarot. It would have made it that much easier!

THERE IS NO "RIGHT" WAY TO READ TAROT

· ✳ ·

The most important thing you need to know about Tarot is that there is no one "right way" to read Tarot.

Yes, breathe a sigh of relief because even though you might have heard some strange rules about Tarot—like you can't buy your own deck or you can't read your own cards—there are no strict guidelines in Tarot.

It all comes down to finding your unique way of connecting with the Tarot cards. It doesn't matter if your way is a little different from how I read the cards or how your friend reads the cards. Ultimately, you need to let *your* intuition guide you about how you want to use the Tarot cards—so long as it is for the Highest Good.

IT'S OK TO INTERPRET THE CARDS IN YOUR OWN SPECIAL WAY

· ✳ ·

Many Tarot beginners worry that they are misinterpreting a Tarot card if it's different from what they read in a book. It's OK if you can't find your interpretation of a card in a Tarot book. In fact, it's awesome because it means that your intuition is kicking into gear. If you're ever unsure if what's speaking to you is your intuition or your ego, go back to the Help! section (see page 45).

TAROT ISN'T JUST ABOUT FORTUNE-TELLING

· ✳ ·

When I first read Tarot, I thought I had to predict the future with 100 percent accuracy to be a good Tarot reader. I would push myself to predict the timing of an event or if something would happen. But every time I tried, I felt like the reading was off and I was missing something more important.

I soon realized that by focusing on the future, I had been missing the opportunities of the present. It is in the present moment where you can make the changes necessary to create the future you most desire.

So I ditched trying to predict the future and instead focused on the present and how I could manifest my goals. And boy, did it change my readings and my life for the better!

Don't fall into the trap of thinking that you need to predict the future to be a good Tarot reader. Focus on where you have the most impact—and for me, that's in the present—and then own it!

YOU DON'T HAVE TO BE A SPIRITUAL MASTER TO ENJOY TAROT

· ✳ ✷ ✳ ·

The Tarot has many connections to deep esoteric systems such as the Kabbalah, astrology, Christianity, Paganism, numerology, mythology, and archetypes. As a Tarot beginner, it's easy to get overwhelmed, thinking that you need to master these systems to appreciate Tarot.

The good news is that you do not need be a spiritual master to benefit from the Tarot cards. Trust your intuition to guide you and know that you don't have to learn everything all at once.

LIVE. LOVE. TAROT.

· ✳ ✷ ✳ ·

Let Tarot be a joyful, lovable part of your life.

Integrate the Tarot into your every day. Experience the magic. And have fun along the way. When you are reading the cards with joy, you are *present*, connecting with your Higher Self, and enriching your life in beautiful ways. And, as we're about to see, you'll make a lot of new discoveries about yourself!

CHAPTER 3

TAROT FOR SELF-DISCOVERY

IT MAY SURPRISE YOU TO KNOW THAT THE WAY I WAS READING TAROT in my twenties differs completely from the way I read Tarot now. Back then I was by the book. I would choose a Tarot reading, form a question (yes, the reverse order to what I teach now), and lay out the cards. Then I'd consult my book to figure out what the reading meant. Sure, I got the insights I needed, but I was just skimming the surface of what the Tarot cards had to tell me.

By my thirties, my method had evolved. I now look at the cards with an open mind and heart and ask, what is this card trying to tell me? I've learned to listen to and trust my own intuition. I look at the imagery and symbolism and use them to open up my connection with my subconscious mind for profound answers. The insights that have come my way have been nothing short of life-changing.

This chapter is where things get exciting. You'll learn how to deepen your self-understanding, discover your soul's purpose, and even heal old wounds and limiting beliefs. Self-discovery is essential, yes, but more than anything this chapter is about building a relationship with your inner, Higher Self.

You have all the answers within you. When you take a moment out of every day just to tune in to your inner wisdom, you can access those answers. It doesn't have to be complicated—just five minutes can be enough!

DAILY TAROT CARD

Most days, I start my morning with a Tarot card. Now, I'm not someone who bounces out of bed to meditate, journal, and do yoga all before the crack of dawn—so don't stress if you're not either! My mornings typically start with one of my daughters running into our bedroom screaming that the other one took her doll and then demanding we make breakfast right now. Not exactly the uber-spiritual morning ritual, right?

But, once the kids are out of the house and at school, I step into my home office—which is also my sacred space—close my eyes, and take in a few deep breaths to ground myself. I think about what I have planned for the day ahead, check in with how I'm feeling, and explore what new possibilities might emerge for me via my intuitive mind.

Then, I open my eyes and pick up my favorite deck, shuffle, and draw a card.

Sometimes I might ask a question, but most times, I'm just checking in with the Tarot and my intuition to see what energy is surrounding me for the day.

I choose the card and then spend some time intuitively exploring the imagery and the energy I receive. What does this card mean to me? What energy do I need to connect with today? How might I make the most out of the hours ahead?

If I have a little extra time, I might start journaling about the card, writing in a stream of consciousness for at least ten minutes.

I'll keep this card top of mind throughout the day, making connections with what's happening and what insight I drew from it. For example, if I draw the Two of Wands, a card about planning for the future, I might dedicate time to

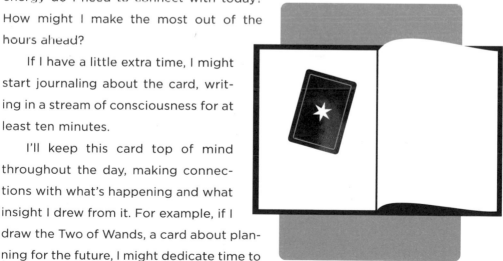

planning my next big project or adventure. If I draw the Chariot, a card about willpower and discipline, and am later faced with the choice to go out with friends or work out at the gym, the card is a good reminder of what is most in alignment with my goals.

Then, in the evening, I'll pull the card out again and reflect on what I've discovered and experienced pertaining to its message.

The next day, I start the process over.

What I love most about the Daily Tarot Card exercise is that it encourages me to make space for myself. It gives me a moment when I can tune in to my inner wisdom and my inner power source to make the most out of the day ahead. It's this little nugget of time that makes the next twenty-four hours oh-so-delicious and aligned.

It's like having a conversation with your Higher Self every single day.

And, if you're learning how to read Tarot, it's the perfect way to pick up what the cards mean through personal experience and intuitive connection.

Self-discovery comes from having a conversation with yourself, just as you would with anyone else you were getting to know better. In that way, the Daily Tarot Card exercise goes well beyond mindfulness; it is the crux of self-discovery through Tarot. And, if you ask me, that makes it one of the most important pieces in the book. Self-discovery builds the trust needed to rely on the intuitive messages that come through the Tarot practices we'll be discussing in the chapters to come.

This is a great time to introduce one of my two favorite ways to connect with my intuition through Tarot: free-flow writing. In fact, I love it so much that I will mention it a lot throughout the rest of this book.

I find free-flow writing to be an excellent and direct way to connect with your subconscious mind—and all the juicy wisdom it holds.

FREE-FLOW WRITING

Gaze at the Tarot card you've pulled for a few minutes and take in what you see. You might also read more about the card's meaning in a book or on www.biddytarot.com.

Then, with a pen and a blank piece of paper, write about that card and what comes up for you when you see its imagery. Keep going for at least ten to fifteen minutes. Keep going even if you have to write something like, "I don't know what to write." Put whatever comes to your mind down on the page and don't judge or correct it. When the time is up, go through your notes and highlight the two to three things that jump out to you most.

Think of free-flow writing as a way of letting your subconscious speak— and I can tell you from experience, what it has to say can surprise and affirm at the same time. I've looked at my writing and felt stunned by what came out of me while at the same time thinking, "Yes, of course, I knew that!" It's in those moments when something "new" feels familiar that your Higher Self is shining through.

These simple exercises not only help you create a personal connection with the Tarot cards; they also give you the opportunity to open up to new possibilities and become more consciously aware of your daily activities, thoughts, and choices. But there are things that can get in the way or gunk up your intuitive works and undermine your trust in what your subconscious is telling you: limiting beliefs. When you do the work of identifying and releasing your limiting beliefs, you'll make it easier for your intuition to speak out loud and clear.

RELEASING LIMITING BELIEFS

If you've read any self-help books, you'll no doubt be familiar with limiting beliefs—those concepts you've developed about yourself that hold you back and impede you living to your fullest potential. They are negative thoughts that you repeat over and over, throughout your lifetime, that reinforce what you know to be possible or impossible.

Limiting beliefs tell you that you'll never find love because all the good ones are taken.

Limiting beliefs explain that you'll never be able to manifest your dream home because all the houses you want are way above your budget.

Limiting beliefs confirm that you'll never be able to work in the top companies because you don't have a degree.

Limiting beliefs undermine your trust in your intuition. Under the influence of a limiting belief, your fear-based ego gets louder and louder and drowns out the voice of your Higher Self, leading you further away from your goals and purpose.

Releasing limiting beliefs is therefore incredibly important if you want to live a "high-vibe" life and stay connected with your inner self. You need to clear out the static, debris, distractions, and noise that garble your intuition and make it harder to hear and trust its voice.

Now, how many times have you heard someone—whether it's a motivational speaker, Oprah, or your therapist—say, "Let go of those limiting beliefs!

Be free!" Meanwhile, you're thinking, "Oh, it's that easy, is it? I have no idea what my limiting beliefs *are*, let alone how to release them!" That's the tricky thing about our limiting beliefs: they're often so intertwined with our thinking we can't see them for what they are. When I initially sat down to pinpoint my limiting beliefs, the best I could come up with was, "I know something is holding me back, but I just can't put my finger on it."

That's where the Tarot cards come in. When it comes to limiting beliefs, the Tarot will help you go beyond that initial feeling of "something is off" to where the action is in your subconscious. The Tarot can help you unlock what is in your subconscious mind, bring it into your conscious awareness, then support you in releasing it and getting on with life.

I tell you, this ain't your grandma's Tarot! Many people have no idea they can use Tarot on such a deep level. Think of it as your secret superpower.

HOW TO DO IT:
RELEASING LIMITING BELIEFS

· ✳ ·

Grab your Tarot cards, a pen, and your journal, and let's get started!

STEP 1:
What Is Bothering You?

Think about your life right now. In what areas of your life are you *not* reaching your goals? Where would you like to see better results?

Write it all down. And if you're a powerfully positive thinker like me and it feels weird to complain, that's okay. Just lean in to this experience of writing everything that's bothering you right now. Don't censor yourself. Don't try to reframe things. Just let it all out, every whingey, whiney word.

STEP 2:
What Limiting Beliefs Are Holding You Back?

Why can't you have what you want?

Take a moment to write what comes to you. Let all those negative thoughts and emotions flow. Give yourself permission to list every excuse under the sun. Be the Negative Nelly! Don't talk yourself out of these beliefs. Just be present with what's coming up for you.

For example, when it comes to my weight, I have a limiting belief that here in my late thirties, losing weight is hard, if not impossible. Another limiting belief reminds me that every time I have followed a food and exercise program, it hasn't worked. Why would this time be any different? So I believe that any kind of weight loss just won't work to begin with or, if it does, it won't stick and it's not worth trying again.

Once you've exhausted your ideas, pull out your Tarot cards to dig even deeper into your limiting beliefs.

You will use the imagery and the messages in the cards to unlock your intuition and subconscious mind about what's holding you back. You'll go beyond what you think you know in your conscious mind and get to the core of what's limiting you.

First, ask your Tarot cards, "What beliefs do I have about [what's bothering you] that are holding me back?"

Draw a card and then take the time to go deep into what it means for you. Set a timer and write continuously for the next ten minutes as you see what comes up for you.

For example, I drew the Nine of Earth from the Gaian Tarot. In the card a beautiful woman is standing in a field of lavender, dressed in a free-flowing robe. This card reminds me that I love the finer things in life, and I feel that I "deserve" to drink wine most evenings and eat at nice restaurants. So my limiting belief might be that I deserve to have what I want in the moment when, ultimately, I know that this is getting in the way of my goals for a healthier body.

After you've explored the first card, draw a second card and see what new insights come up for you. For my second card, I drew the Three of Earth reversed. This card shows three women cooking in the kitchen with fresh produce from the garden, as they laugh and share stories with each other. Reversed, this card suggests I'm worried that if I do embark on a more healthy lifestyle, I won't be able to cook my favorite foods and won't enjoy my time in the kitchen as much as I do now.

If you slip from identifying your limiting beliefs to creating the solution for overcoming them, note your ideas and come back to them later. It's not the time to go into "solution mode" just yet.

Finally, summarize your limiting beliefs on a separate piece of paper.

STEP 3:
Question Your Beliefs

For each of your limiting beliefs, acknowledge that they are merely thoughts, not truths or facts.

To support the process of letting them go, run each belief through the following questions. Note your initial response and then draw a Tarot card for each question to help you dig deeper.

Limiting Belief: _____

1. On what basis do I believe this to be true?

2. What is the origin of this belief?

3. What benefit do I gain from keeping this belief?

4. How does this belief limit my potential?

5. What might I experience if I were to let go of this belief?

Once you have answered the five questions, check in with yourself again about the limiting belief. Ask yourself, "Do I still believe this to be true?" You might find that you do. If so, go over the five questions again. Or you may feel that the energy around the belief has dissipated and you no longer subscribe to it. Hooray! You're free!

It's a wonderful thing to feel the weight of your limiting beliefs lift off your shoulders. Sometimes, however, the source of your limiting beliefs is something much bigger. Long-held wounds, fears, or deeply felt pain require more than just conscious attention. You have to heal before you can let go.

SELF-HEALING WITH TAROT

I once had a client—let's call her Rebecca—who was going through a rough time in her relationship. She was trying to open up to her partner and share

what was happening to her at work, but she didn't feel like he heard her and gave her the attention she needed. She could feel her inner power and strength shriveling up every time she interacted with him.

Rebecca knew something had to change, and she wasn't ready to walk away from this relationship just yet. So in our session together we flipped through the Tarot deck to find a card that resonated with her and the energy she wanted to bring into her relationship, and support within herself.

After going through the deck a few times, Rebecca landed on the Strength card. She knew in her gut that this was the card that would help her heal her inner wounds around speaking her truth and "being strong from within," as she put it.

Over the next few months, Rebecca carried the Strength card around with her, and every day she connected with the card to draw in its energy. She noticed things about the card, such as how this beautiful woman could cradle the ferocious lion, and it showed her new aspects of herself that she hadn't seen before. She realized that she had more power and control in her relationship, especially if she could engage with her partner from a place of inner strength.

The Tarot card became her way of healing old wounds and reinstalling the energy of the card within her psyche so that she could create a better relationship with her partner.

When she checked in with me three months later, things had changed for the better. Rebecca was having more empowered conversations with her partner, and she had an inner knowing that she didn't need to have his attention all the time. She could get that from within. It was just icing on the cake to have her partner reinforce her strength.

Many people believe that the Tarot cards will tell you what's going on. But do you realize that you can use the cards more proactively to heal what you need to heal?

HOW TO DO IT: TAROT FOR SELF-HEALING
· * ✷ * ·

If you are working on a personal issue or concern, the Tarot can help you manifest the energy you need to get things back on track. It's as simple as selecting a Tarot card that embodies either your current issue or concern, or your desired state, and working with this card.

STEP 1:
Focus on What You Want to Heal

Ask yourself, "What aspect of my life needs healing right now?" If you're hit with a flood of issues, just choose one. And if you get stuck, why not pull out your Tarot cards and ask?

Write out your issue, and give yourself permission to let it all out. Complain, whine, get angry—anything you need.

STEP 2:
Consciously Choose a Tarot Card

Once you're clear on what's bothering you, go through your Tarot deck and consciously select a card you feel would be helpful to you right now in healing this issue.

You might start by selecting five or six cards and then narrow it down to just one.

If you get stuck, ask your intuition to guide you: let your hand hover over the cards and then choose the one that gives you the most energy.

Take a moment to write why you've selected the card that you have.

For example, if you were struggling with overeating, you might work with the Nine of Cups, which can be associated with greed and immediate satisfaction at one end of the scale and general contentment and happiness at the other. Your focus may be on how to move into healthier eating habits that still allow you to have what you want . . . just in moderation.

STEP 3:
Work with the Tarot Card

There are many ways to work with a Tarot card for self-healing. Free-flow writing is one of my favorites. The other is meditating with the Tarot card.

A quick confession: I've never been great at "regular" meditation. With no place for my mind to go, it doesn't take long for my body to get squirmy. But meditating with a Tarot card? That I can do. It's as though my intuition has delivered my mind a playground, somewhere to engage, explore, and discover. Much like free-flow writing, you will see meditation popping up in a lot of our activities in this book. I hope you love it as much as I do!

MEDITATE WITH THE TAROT CARD

Gaze at the Tarot card for a few minutes and let the imagery flow into your mind.

Then, close your eyes and take a few deep breaths. Ground your energy and bring your attention to your body, gently clearing your mind of any thoughts.

In your mind's eye, bring up the image of the Tarot card you've just been looking at. Flesh it out all nice and big, in full color and 3D, as though it's a movie scene. Take a moment to pay attention to the energy you feel when you see it. What do you notice? How do you feel?

Now, imagine you were stepping into this movie and becoming a part of the scene itself. Become the character on the card. Step into their shoes. Feel the sensation of the clothes on your skin. Take a deep breath in and smell the surrounding air. You might even taste something. Let it be a full sensory experience. Now, what do you notice? And what do you feel? How can you bring this energy into your everyday life to heal your wounds and create the outcomes you want?

Now, step out of character, but stay within the movie scene. Turn to the character from this card and ask, "What guidance do you have for me?" You might hear something. You might be shown something or find that you suddenly know something. Or you might experience nothing at all. It's all okay. Just have an open, curious mind.

As you get ready to leave the card and the scene, thank your guide. Then step out of the movie scene and imagine it getting smaller and smaller, fading away and becoming grey, until it is nothing but a tiny dot.

Open your eyes, then write about everything that you experienced during the visualization.

Again, you may feel complete after this one experience, or you may want to do this meditation several times to strengthen the energy of the card and your healing process.

The better you can "hear" what your intuition has to say, the better it can guide you. Ultimately, however, the discoveries you make through an intuitive connection via the Tarot will be things you already know—or at least your inner self does. Exploring areas of your life, and anything you want to heal or create through meditation or free-flow writing, can yield some amazing and impactful discoveries—including one of the biggest and most impactful discoveries of all.

DISCOVERING YOUR SOUL PURPOSE

One thing people often say about me is that I am very soul-driven. I know why I'm here and how I can serve others in this lifetime—and I'm making it happen every day.

For me, understanding my soul purpose is something that happens on a day-to-day basis. Every day, I'm learning something new about myself and continually making changes to realign with my soul's purpose. It's a constant feedback loop of trying something, seeing if it resonates, and then either doing more of it or trying something different.

But if I were to pinpoint an exact moment when my soul's purpose became clearer than it has ever been, it would be during a moving meditation to Rage Against the Machine's "Killing in the Name Of." That experience came when I was questioning whether I wanted to continue Biddy Tarot. My energy was fading, and I was getting bored—a sign that something wasn't right. But once I connected on a deep, soul level to what I had been sent here to do, there was no denying it. I had to keep going with Biddy Tarot because I had a special job to do.

That's the thing with knowing your soul purpose: it feels as if you must follow your calling, because if you don't, you're doing a disservice to the Higher Power and the people on this planet. There are no other options but to follow your path.

WHAT IS A SOUL PURPOSE?

· * ✳ * ·

Your soul purpose is the reason you are here on this earth, in this lifetime. It represents the lessons you learn and what you are here to teach others.

Your soul purpose gives you direction on a deep, fundamental level. It is your "calling," your guiding light. It's what gets you up every day and drives you forward with divine determination and will.

When you discover your soul purpose, you align with your highest power and creativity and can manifest your deepest desires into your world. This purpose expands your heart and mind, opening you to experience the amazing multidimensional being that you are.

Soul purpose is powerful stuff.

But here's an essential thing to keep in mind: your soul purpose is dynamic. It can change, grow, and evolve—just as you do. And here's the truth: you already know your soul purpose even if you think you don't. Your soul purpose is at the core of you and your being. It is not something you need to "find."

Linda thought there was something wrong with her because she couldn't pinpoint her soul purpose. But as she says, "Now that I'm older, I have come to realize that my soul purpose is doing what truly fulfills me in that moment, whether it's being a mum, an artist, a construction worker, a Tarot reader—you name it! Just as the seasons change, life changes and our purpose changes too."

For some people, their soul purpose comes through as an epiphany in a moment in time, similar to the meditation experience I had. For others, it's a gentler process, trusting their intuition and being guided to the right path, even if that "right path" changes. Others will have multiple soul purposes, like stepping-stones, evolving each time.

When you have a deep connection with your inner self, you become more consciously aware of this larger purpose.

It is at the moment we let go and trust in the wider Universe and the Universe within that life guides us forward and we open up fully to the present moment. We discover our passion and desire for life again, which brings our soul purpose and mission back to the fore.

But here's the thing—it's not enough to just discover your soul purpose and be done with it. When you know why you're here, it's your responsibility and your obligation to the Universe to follow through with your purpose and live it in your everyday life. That means saying yes to opportunities in alignment with your purpose and saying no to those that are not.

Sometimes being clear on your soul purpose acts as a litmus test or a guiding light. When faced with a difficult decision or a fork in the road, your soul's mission is so powerful it will illuminate the path for your future so you can always see which direction to take.

This is why practices like meditation, journaling, and Tarot card reading are so important. They create the sacred space for you to reconnect with your inner being and your soul's purpose. They help you stay in alignment with the reason you're here.

So how do you know what your soul purpose is? Your soul is always calling to you. It calls to you through whispers, subtle symbols and signs, and deep yearnings. It makes its presence known through your enthusiasm, passion, and excitement and through your frustration, resistance, and anger. You start to discover your soul purpose when you open yourself to new opportunities with a curious mind and you find what lights you up— and what doesn't.

My approach to soul alignment has always been to do it and see how it feels. If it feels good, keep doing it. If it feels bad, stop doing it. And over time, you start to find what is in alignment with what you need.

When you follow what lights you up, you are working with who you are and in flow with the Universe. You are living the life you were born to live *and*, even better, the life that *only you* can live. And that's a powerful thing.

So how do you bring this powerful drive into your conscious awareness? Well, I have a little something for that . . .

THE SOUL PURPOSE TAROT READING
· ∗ ✦ ∗ ·

The Soul Purpose Tarot Reading is a potent experience designed to help you uncover the layers of your soul purpose so that you can live every day in alignment with your Higher Self.

Now, will this reading tell you exactly what your soul purpose is, down to the last detail? No, that is up to you to explore and discover. But it will give you guidance, a path forward, signposts and bread crumbs on your trail toward determining what lights you up.

Do this reading every so often—not every week!—and combine it with other regular practices such as meditation and journaling to deepen its effect and explore what it means for you.

The reading starts with a little "soul dreaming," dreaming big about the possibilities available to you. Then it follows up with a ten-card spread. Lastly, there's a little homework so you can explore your insights.

STEP 1:
Soul Dreaming

Let's begin by first creating the sacred dreaming space for discovering your soul's purpose. Imagine that, for the next year, you have unlimited access to all the money, love, creativity, and time that your heart desires. There is no limit to what you can be, do, have, experience, and create in your life. Here is your opportunity to go for it and live out all of your wildest dreams.

Now take time to sit down and write in great detail precisely what you will be, do, have, experience, and manifest in the year ahead. Dream big!

When you're brainstorming, remember there are no right or wrong answers, and your journey is individual and unique. You don't have to be like other people or create what you think others want you to create. This is *your* journey.

Also, be consciously aware of your energy during this soul dreaming pro-cess. What lights you up? What makes your heart burst when you think about it? When do you feel fear creep in? These are all clues as to your soul purpose.

See your soul purpose take shape.

STEP 2:
The Soul Purpose Tarot Spread

To deepen your understanding of your soul purpose, pull out your Tarot deck to do the Soul Purpose reading. As you start this reading, take a moment to center yourself. Find a quiet place and, holding your Tarot cards, gently close your eyes. Take a deep breath in and replace any tension with relaxation. Turn your attention inward. Give yourself permission to spend time with yourself—right here, right now.

Open your eyes. You are now ready for the reading. Shuffle the cards, focusing on your soul dreaming, and, when you are ready, lay them out using the following spread:

1	2	3
What aspect of yourself are you expressing in this present moment?	What aspect of your soul wants to be expressed?	How can you create alignment between you and your soul?

4	5	6	7
What life lessons and themes did you choose to explore in this lifetime?	What challenges are you here to experience?	What are your greatest gifts, talents, or potential?	How can you best manifest your potential?

8	9	10
What is your personal soul purpose (what you came to accomplish on an individual level)?	What is your global community soul purpose (what you came to accomplish on a global level)?	What steps can you take to bring your soul purpose into your everyday life?

Lay out the cards and take time to go through each one, connecting with your intuition and your soul throughout the reading. Pay attention to the balance of upright and reversed cards, knowing that reversed cards show your inner workings and upright cards reflect how you express yourself to the world.

Take a photo of the reading and write your insights in your Tarot journal or notebook. This is *big* stuff right here, so allow a good amount of time to dive into the cards and explore their messages for you. Come back to the reading over the next few days and weeks, and you'll find that it continues to unfold and open up to you even more.

THE SOUL ALIGNMENT CHECK-IN

When I was twelve, I went yacht racing with my dad every Sunday. At first, I thought it'd be easy; just set the sails, line up the rudder, and away you go. But what I realized is that to navigate the fastest and most efficient route, we needed to check the wind direction and speed, tweak the sails, adjust the steering, watch for big waves, keep out of the way of oncoming seacraft, and so on, all while making sure the yacht was heading toward the finish line.

Living your soul purpose is very similar. You can't "set it and forget it" once you know what your purpose is. Instead, you need to check that you're in alignment with it on a day-to-day basis.

Given that my soul purpose is expressed mostly through my work, I am always making sure that what I'm doing is in alignment with my Higher Self. For example, when I have a new business idea, I stop and check in to see if it resonates and is worth pursuing. First, I'll check in intuitively. I'll envision the idea in my mind and step into what it would feel like if I were doing that idea. I get a sense of how it feels, whether I'm excited by it, and if it has the potential to lead to new opportunities. Then, I get out my Tarot cards and ask for guidance on soul alignment.

The Soul Alignment Check-In can work with any new opportunity in your life: hobbies, travel, training and courses, relationships—you name it. Use it whenever you want to know if something is in alignment with your soul purpose in this lifetime.

HOW TO DO IT: SOUL ALIGNMENT CHECK-IN

STEP 1:
Intuitively Connect with Your Idea

Close your eyes and take a few deep breaths. Ground your energy and bring your attention to your body, clearing your mind of any thoughts.

Follow the same technique you would use to meditate with a Tarot card, but this time, step into your idea.

When you're ready, gently open your eyes and write down your experiences. Ask yourself, from this experience alone, "Does this new idea align with my soul purpose?"

STEP 2:
Do the Soul Alignment Check-In Tarot Reading

Now, with your idea still in your mind, ask your Tarot cards for guidance on whether it is in alignment with your soul purpose.

Use this simple five-card Soul Alignment Check-In Spread:

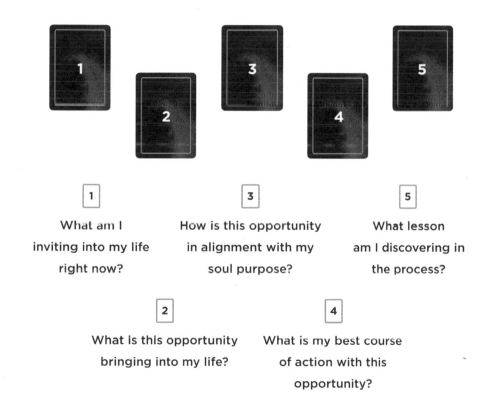

1	3	5
What am I inviting into my life right now?	How is this opportunity in alignment with my soul purpose?	What lesson am I discovering in the process?

2	4
What is this opportunity bringing into my life?	What is my best course of action with this opportunity?

Don't expect the cards to give you a clear yes or no about whether this opportunity is in alignment with your soul purpose. You might find that the message you receive is a little vague and you will need to do the work to understand if it's the right fit for you. The cards will give you some clues, but the rest is up to you! (Thank you, free will!)

The work you'll do in this chapter is perhaps the most important of this entire book. As you build trust in your inner wisdom, strengthen your intuitive connection, and live in alignment with your soul purpose, you'll step into your power to create the life you want. No goal will be out of reach!

CHAPTER 4

MANIFEST YOUR GOALS

A LOT OF PEOPLE BELIEVE THE TAROT HELPS THEM **TELL** THEIR FUTURE.

But I believe something very different: I believe the Tarot helps you *create* your future.

By supercharging your vision of what's possible and aligning your goals with your soul purpose, you can bring your dreams into reality.

It's powerful stuff, right?

In this chapter, I'll show you how to take what you truly want and use the Tarot cards and your intuition to manifest it.

This doesn't mean I don't believe in traditional goal setting and planning strategies—I do. But I've discovered that if you set goals without first tapping into your intuition, they often fall by the wayside. However, when you map out goals *and* connect them with your intuition, you take your manifestation abilities to superstar levels and get amazing results.

In the pages to come, I'll show you how to use the Tarot to create intuitively inspired goals, plan your path, and manifest your dreams.

INTUITIVELY INSPIRED GOALS

Back in 2012, my family manifested our dream holiday: a six-month adventure in Spain. We traveled around, lived in small towns, and experienced the local culture. I worked remotely while exploring new places and spending quality time with my family.

One day I was working at a picnic table near the beach with my laptop and *café con hielo*. As I looked out at the shimmering blue water, I started envisioning what I wanted my business to look like in the next twelve months. I had made some amazing things happen for myself, but I wanted to get more intentional about my next steps and goals.

The year before, I had created an income of $100,000 through my Tarot business alone—which was pretty awesome given that this is what I had been earning when I left my corporate job. But, being the high achiever I am, I was ready to go to the next level.

I wanted to set my financial goal for the year ahead. I could aim to make the same amount. Or I could reach for $150,000, an increase that felt achievable. Or I could double my income to $200,000, a thought that sent a jolt of excitement through my body.

Now, of course, it's not all about the money. There's no point in manifesting a million dollars when it all comes at the expense of spending time with loved ones or working ninety-hour weeks. As I thought about my financial goal, I wanted to be sure it would also allow me to sustain and even improve the lifestyle I had created—meaning lots of travel and time with my family!

Then I did what any normal, modern-day mystic would do: I pulled out my Tarot cards.

For each income goal I had in mind, I drew a Tarot card and placed it next to the written goal. As I pulled each card, I asked the question:

"Is this goal in alignment with my Highest Good?"

For the $100,000, I drew the Four of Cups. This card shows a guy sitting underneath a tree. Even though there's a cup being offered to him and three more in front of him, he doesn't seem too interested. In fact, he looks downright bored and over it.

When it came to my goal of $100,000, the Four of Cups suggested that it was an achievable goal, but one I might become bored or disinterested in. That resonated with me. As soon as I saw the card, my intuition told me that my overachieving mind and my Higher Self were asking for more. So I moved on to the next choice.

For $150,000, I drew the Page of Swords, a young guy holding his sword toward the sky. As a Page, he's learning something new, and as a Sword card, he's focused on communication and the intellect. So, this card was telling me that the goal of $150,000 was interesting enough to keep me engaged intellectually and would probably offer new opportunities to communicate with my audience. However, a Page is not as mature or developed as a Queen or a King, so I had a hunch that my Higher Self was capable of more.

For $200,000, I drew the Eight of Pentacles, featuring a man working hard, etching pentacles into a series of disks. He's meticulous as he focuses on making each disk the same, and his work is beginning to pay off. From this, I knew that it would take hard work and determination to make $200,000, but the effort would be worthwhile. I felt my energy level rising, and could tell I was in tune with my intuition.

Just for kicks, I scribbled down $250,000 and pulled another card: the Queen of Pentacles. *Oh, yes!* This Queen is the quintessential female entrepreneur who not only has her business in order but also her family—and managing my work and family commitments in a balanced way is critically important to me. This was feeling both exciting *and* achievable.

I felt inspired to see if I could take it even a little further (thank you, high-achieving brain). I wrote down $300,000 and drew a big circle around the number. I pulled the Ten of Cups reversed. *Ah!* We had reached the breaking point. Upright, the Ten of Cups is all about harmony at home: a happy family, a happy partner, a happy home life. But reversed, it suggests that this happy home life is all out of balance. Because family and lifestyle are so important to me, I knew that I wasn't willing to chase a financial goal at the expense of my personal life. That was something I refused to sacrifice.

I looked back at my goals and the cards I had pulled and was thrilled to see my income goal for 2013: $250,000! If I hadn't turned to the cards to guide me through this process, I probably would have stopped at $150,000 or $200,000. But now I had a healthy goal, backed with my intuition and the energy of my Higher Self, and the inspiration to achieve it.

(In case you're wondering, I hit that goal in 2013—with another $20,000 to boot, and I was able to spend another six months in Spain with my family!)

Don't settle for what you *think*. Check in with your intuition and *feel* what is possible. Connect with Universal energy and lean in to your inner wisdom to fulfill your highest potential.

Let's create an intuitively inspired goal together, right here, right now.

STEP 1:
DREAM BIG
· * ✳ * ·

Close your eyes and call up your wildest dreams and goals.

What is it that you want to create?

Visualize it. Imagine your dream playing out as if it were on a movie screen in your mind.

Feel it. Pay attention to your emotions and feelings as you watch your dream come to life. Feel the excitement, the inspiration, the motivation, even the tingles of fear.

Notice where your dreams arise within your body. Do you feel your heart swelling with happiness? Is your chest rising with pride? Are butterflies of excitement filling your stomach?

You can use your Tarot cards for extra depth here. You might ask, "What is coming into my conscious awareness about my wildest dreams?" Then pull a card. What you're looking for here is an intuitive clue or even some validation of your vision and your dreams.

For example, you might draw the Seven of Pentacles, a sign that your goals and dreams will need a sustained focus over time. Or you might draw the Hermit, a sign that you'll be walking this path alone and it is an important part of your spiritual journey.

How does the card move you?

STEP 2:
CREATE YOUR STRETCH GOAL
· ✳ ★ ✳ ·

Once you're within your big dream, it's time to create your stretch goal.

How would you describe your wildest dream in one sentence?

Write it down.

Don't worry if your stretch goal feels out of reach or even a little scary. That's the idea! If we hold ourselves back from imagining our wildest dreams, we don't even allow for the possibility that they *could* happen. Let yourself dream big.

While the stretch goal isn't necessarily the goal you'll use for manifesting, it sets the scene for the SMART goal you'll create next.

STEP 3:
CREATE YOUR SMART GOAL

· ✳ ✴ ✳ ·

SMART goals are designed to help you take your big, beautiful dream and turn it into something real and achievable, using a concrete plan of action.

Break down your stretch goal and turn it into something that is specific, meaningful, agreed-upon, realistic, and time-based. Answer the following questions:

✴ **What do you want to create? Be Specific.**

✴ **Why do you want to create it? Make it Meaningful.**

✴ **Are you committed? Agree on your goal.**

✴ **Is your goal achievable? Make it Realistic.**

✴ **When will you create it? Give it a Time frame.**

For example, if your stretch goal is to become the queen of macramé and decorate your home with your artwork, your SMART goal might be, "By July, I will learn how to create my first wall-hanging, and by the end of the year, my home will be filled with at least five beautiful macramé works of art."

As you're creating your SMART goal, you're using your rational mind, gathering data, researching information, and assessing what's possible based on the information you have. Your intuition may chime in, but this is your rational mind's opportunity to shine. Later, when you calibrate your goal with your intuition, you may find that the goal changes.

STEP 4:
INTUITIVELY CALIBRATE YOUR GOALS

· ✳ ✴ ✳ ·

Here's where you go to the next level and align your goals with your Highest Good.

Look at your SMART goal and ask your Higher Self, "To what extent is this goal in alignment with my Highest Good?" Draw a Tarot card to support you in this process.

You might find that your SMART goal is too safe and you're playing small. In this case, set a bigger goal and check in with the cards again until you find your sweet spot.

Or you might find that your goal is exciting, but out of alignment with what you truly desire. For example, you might be able to achieve it, but to the detriment of your relationships, career, or personal well-being. If this is the case, then scale it back until you find that sweet spot again, using your cards and your intuition throughout the process.

STEP 5:
FINALIZE YOUR INTUITIVELY INSPIRED GOAL
· ✳ ✴ ✳ ·

Once you have your final, revised SMART goal, tune in to your intuition and once again ask yourself, "To what extent is my goal in alignment with my Highest Good?" Focus your attention within and check in to see how you're feeling about your goal.

You can also say your goal out loud and listen carefully to how it resonates with you. Do you find yourself holding back or whispering as you say it? Or can you state your goal with confidence and pride?

If something still feels a little off, go back to Step 4 and recalibrate your goals with your intuition.

Once you've landed on your inspired goal, write it down and stick it up in a visible place.

To help make this easy for you, I've created a bonus worksheet inside of the Reader Resources—you'll find it at www.everydaytarot.com.

In the next section, I'll show you how to turn this goal into a reality.

POWERFUL MANIFESTATION

It's time to powerfully manifest your goals and dreams, using your intuition and the Tarot cards as your guide.

In a traditional planning process, you would take your SMART goal and break down the steps you need to bring that goal to fruition. This is still an essential part of manifesting your goals, so don't skip it.

But there's another step to take first.

Before you start planning and taking action, use your Tarot cards to connect to your intuition and discover the most effective way to go about manifesting your goals. *Then* create your action plan.

This vital step is why I created the Manifestation Tarot Spread, an eleven-card Tarot reading that will show you what you need to do to turn your dreams into reality.

I've used this spread to supercharge my business and personal goals with great results. For example, every year I retreat for several days to set my business goals and create my action plan and strategy for the year ahead. Once I set my goals, I do the Manifestation Tarot Spread to intuitively align with my goal and tune in to my Higher Self before I create my action plan and strategy. Even though I *think* I know what I need to do, I always find that this Manifestation reading shifts my thinking up a level, and I create something even better and more aligned with my purpose.

THE MANIFESTATION TAROT SPREAD

· ✳ ·

With your intuitively inspired goal in mind, shuffle the Tarot cards and then lay out the cards using this eleven-card spread.

1	2	3	4
How am I feeling about my goal?	What is the true potential if I manifest this goal?	What do I need to release to manifest my goal?	What do I need to create to manifest my goal?

5	6	7

What are my next steps?

(Pull three cards, one for each potential step.)

8

What lesson do I need to master?

9	10	11

If I stay committed to my goal, what might I experience over the next three/six/twelve months?

(Pull three cards, one for each time period.)

Now, let's break it down, card by card.

CARD 1:
How Am I Feeling about My Goal?

This card indicates your connection with your goal in the present moment.

If this card shows a positive, energized relationship with your goal, that's great! You're set to go!

However, if this card shows a negative relationship with your goal, you may need to work through any self-doubt or fear before taking action.

That doesn't mean you can't move ahead with creating your dream. But it does bring your awareness to any reservations or struggles you may be experiencing. Luckily, being conscious of reservations or doubts can help clear out that energy and make way for an unclouded path ahead.

In our example, Card 1 is the Knight of Wands, a card filled with inspiration, motivation, and energy. What's great about this card is that it aligns with the energy of the Eight of Wands, the card we drew when we were evaluating the goal. There's a ton of inspired energy here and you're raring to go!

CARD 2:

What Is the True Potential If I Manifest this Goal?

This card shows you what's possible if you go for it and make your dream a reality.

If you've done the work of creating intuitively inspired goals, then this card will likely show a positive outcome and act as another green light to encourage you to move forward. It's a sign that the true potential of achieving this goal is huge.

If you draw a card that shows an undesirable outcome, then it's time to go back to the drawing board and recalibrate your goals with your Highest Good. Find the goal that is going to lead to the best possible outcome.

Now, take a quick look back at Card 1. If Card 1 shows that you have some doubts or reservations, but Card 2 shows a positive outcome, then you need to focus on where your goal is leading you and get energized to overcome those initial nerves!

In our example, Card 2 is the Judgement card. At first glance, you might feel a little worried—are you going to be judged by the higher powers!? Dig a little deeper. What do you see?

In the Judgement card, we see people standing up in their graves, arms reaching to the skies. It's a little morbid, yes, but there is a powerful underlying message here: you are being called to something greater, and by focusing on your goal and manifesting your dreams, you'll step into a whole new level of human potential. Exciting, huh!?

CARD 3:
What Do I Need to Release to Manifest My Goal?

What got you here won't get you there. That is, you can't continue to do the same things you've always done before if you expect to see different results. A change in approach is needed.

This card will guide you to discover what you need to let go of so new energy can shine through. It can also show you what you need to stop doing: a habit or practice that may be getting in the way of your success.

Card 3 in our example reading is the Eight of Swords. In this card, we see a blindfolded woman, apparently trapped and bound between eight swords. I say "apparently" because there *is* a way out—the woman just can't see it because she's blindfolded. This is a card often associated with limiting beliefs that are holding you back.

While Card 1 shows that you're raring to go and filled with inspiration, Card 3 is reminding you that in order to give yourself the best opportunity at achieving your goal, you'll need to release any limiting beliefs that may be getting in the way.

CARD 4:
What Do I Need to Create to Manifest My Goal?

Just as you will need to release something to manifest your goal, you will also need to bring new energy into your life. This card shows you what you need to nurture and grow to reach your goal.

In our example, Card 4 is the Six of Wands. In this card, there's a man proudly riding on his horse while the people around him cheer him on. This card holds a great sense of confidence and achievement. So when it comes to what you need to create, you need to bring more of this confident energy into your life! That's a beautiful transition away from the limiting Eight of Swords and toward the confidence of the Six of Wands.

CARDS 5-7:
What Are My Next Steps?

The next three cards show you the steps you need to take to manifest your goals.

Typically, these cards are read in chronological order: Card 5 shows you the first step; Card 6, the second step; and Card 7, the third.

You may also notice some interesting patterns or a flow as you interpret these cards from left to right. For example, is there a common symbol between the cards? How does this symbol change and evolve from one card to the next? This may give you more information about your next steps.

These three action cards should work hand in hand with your traditional planning process. They don't *replace* traditional planning, but instead offer you additional intuitive information to keep in mind as you create your plan.

Let's take a look at the cards in the example spread—Two of Swords, Seven of Cups, and the Chariot.

The Two of Swords typically represents a challenging decision that you know you must make but you're reluctant to because you don't have all the information you need. Notice the blindfold is showing up again, just like in the Eight of Swords. So the first step may be to remove your metaphorical blindfold, clear those limiting beliefs, and then make this decision that has been lingering for a while.

With the Seven of Cups, we see a man presented with seven cups filled with various items. Some of the items are desirable—like jewels—but others are not—snakes and dragons. So after you've lifted the blindfold and made that challenging decision, it's time to evaluate your options and make sure you're taking the opportunity that offers you the most value

Finally, the Chariot shows a charioteer steering forward, even though the black and white sphinxes appear to be pulling in different directions. This card is all about willpower and self-discipline, so once you have your options in front of you, it's time to choose one and commit to it with dogged determination.

CARD 8:
What Lesson Do I Need to Master?

When we're in manifesting mode, the beautiful thing is that we're not just creating something new; we're also evolving and growing as people. So Card 8 taps into the personal lesson you're mastering as you manifest your goal.

If this is a Major Arcana card, then you are blessed with the opportunity of learning a major life lesson. If it is a Minor Arcana card, then the lesson may be more practical or temporary. And if it is a Court Card, then you may

see a new aspect of yourself as you progress with your goal. Pay attention to decipher the specific lesson for you.

In our example, Card 8 is the Empress, a beautiful, pregnant woman seated on a velvet lounge, surrounded by flowers, fruit, and nature. The word that I most associate with the Empress is "abundance." She lives this abundant lifestyle and has everything she needs to enjoy life for what it is. And so with this card, the lesson to be mastered is that of abundance. How can you accept and embrace abundance as you manifest this goal?

We can take it one step further and relate the Empress back to the limiting beliefs of the Eight of Swords. Perhaps those limiting beliefs have to do with abundance and, as you manifest this goal, you'll let go of the belief that you are not worthy.

CARDS 9–11:
If I Stay Committed to My Goal, What Might I Experience over the Next Three/Six/Twelve Months?

We all like to see what's possible in the future. With these three cards, you're gaining insight into what you *might* experience in the future if you commit to your goal. Note how I said "might." Your future is not set in stone, despite what some people might have you believe about Tarot. What you see here is more of a reflection of where you are right now and where you could be heading, rather than what will definitely happen.

If you find that the cards show an undesirable flow of future events, don't let it get you down. Remember, forewarned is forearmed. If you see a message here that you don't want, you can always take action and turn it into something you *do* want. Or you can prepare yourself for what's to come. For instance, if the ninth card indicates that business could be slow for the first three months of the year, but the tenth card is all about abundance, you'll know to put your head down and get through the early months to see results. You may need to shift your path or change your mindset based on what you see here. But remember, you have the power to create what you want.

In the example reading, Cards 9–11 are the Page of Pentacles, Nine of Wands, and Nine of Pentacles.

The Page of Pentacles shows a young man holding up a coin. He's ready and willing to explore financial matters and is often associated with learning the ropes of business. This card suggests that you'll first go through a phase of learning more about business and how to manage your finances so that you can reach your goal and attract new clients.

In the Nine of Wands, a heavily bandaged man stands exhausted in front of a row of wands. He's gone through a rough patch, but the good thing is he's still standing. So while you may face a few challenges along your path, you have the resilience to keep persevering and pushing on. This is also when the energy of the Chariot will motivate you and keep you going.

Finally, the Nine of Pentacles is a very positive sign that everything will work out in the end. This card shows a woman standing in a beautiful garden, surrounded by luscious vines and flowers. It has many similarities to the Empress, with its energy of abundance and luxury, and is a positive sign that not only will you achieve the goal; you'll also master the lesson of abundance along the way. That may be the secret to your success right there—abundance!

CONNECT WITH THE
ENERGY OF THE TAROT

Now that you have your intuitively inspired SMART goal and have mapped your path to manifestation, it's time to connect with the energy of the Tarot cards to infuse your path with even more success.

Yes, the Tarot cards can be an energy source. The symbolism, story, and archetypes of Tarot lend themselves to building a desired energy within you that you can harness in positive and proactive ways. It works a little like magic, in the truest sense of the word.

Of course, you can play with this energy in whichever way calls to you, but as we discussed in chapter 3, meditating with the Tarot cards and free writing are powerful ways to connect with the Tarot, your intuition, and, yes, the Universe to bring your dream into reality. No matter your method, the important thing is that you engage with your goal, keeping it top of mind and infusing it with the powerful energy of your intention.

Manifestation is not a one-off activity, but should instead be a regular practice or interaction. By keeping your soul purpose and intuitively inspired goals at the center of your thinking, you will be better equipped to confidently make decisions.

CHAPTER 5

TAROT FOR DECISION-MAKING

MOVING TO A NEW NEIGHBORHOOD, CHANGING JOBS, LEAVING A long-term relationship, starting a business—life is full of decisions, big and small. And every decision you make can take your life in a new or different direction. Put together, your decisions carve out your life's path.

For some of us, big decisions equal big opportunities. When you make that grand, bold move to change careers, your choice opens new possibilities and fills you up with a renewed sense of energy and inspiration.

But for other others, decisions can overwhelm or even paralyze them. "How do I know what to choose?" they wonder. "What if I make the wrong choice?" Some of us prefer to avoid the decision, bury our heads in the sand, and hope it will pass. The sad thing is that this inaction—or lack of intentional action—can limit our personal growth and progress. If you don't decide, you'll end up doing the same thing you always have and not making any bold moves in your life. But if you make decisions *consciously* and in alignment with your soul purpose, you can create the outcomes you want.

In this chapter, we'll discuss how to use the Tarot to find much-needed clarity when facing a big decision. I'll show you how to explore your options, feel good about your choices, and receive guidance—without sacrificing your free will! But first, let's talk about why big decisions need more than a simple yes or no. Your intuition is a powerful compass, but it shouldn't be the only piece of information you take into consideration.

A POWERFUL COMPASS

I've faced many big decisions in my life that affect not only me but my family too. One of the biggest was the move with my husband and daughters to an entirely new state, leaving behind our loved ones.

I had lived in Melbourne, Australia, for most of my life. But my husband and I had become increasingly restless living in a big city. Surrounded by houses, traffic, and the general hustle and bustle of metropolitan living, we craved nature. We wanted a warm environment, with fewer people, more space, and the relaxed lifestyle that comes with those things.

So we explored whether it was the right time for our family to move—and not just somewhere in the outskirts of Melbourne, but a relocation up north.

We spent three weeks visiting different parts of the Australian East Coast to see what might be a good fit for us. When we visited the Sunshine Coast, with its pristine beaches, warm weather year-round, and luscious rainforest, we knew we wanted to live there. But, that didn't make it easy. Our two young daughters loved spending time with their grandparents and cousins in Melbourne, and we would be taking them a plane-ride away. And we worried that we'd miss our friends and many of the fun aspects of city living, such as good food, culture, and events. I couldn't imagine leaving.

But I also couldn't deny this thought bubbling up from within saying we needed a change and we needed it *soon*.

Here's the thing: We could have just stayed in Melbourne, kept our families happy, and continued with the lives we had created there. We could have maintained the status quo, and we would have been fine! But there was something else calling us—something big. And we listened to that call. Sure, we had no friends or family on the Sunshine Coast. And, yes, we had only spent a week there and had no clue if it suited our needs. Were we acting on a whim? Maybe it looked that way from the outside. But Anthony and I knew we were acting on our souls' calling.

It was a big transition, but it paid off. We found our gorgeous, resort-style home, surrounded by five acres of rainforest, and enjoy a much more "chill" lifestyle now that we're out of the city. We could not be happier! Do we miss our friends and family? Absolutely. But had we stayed in Melbourne, our energy would have drained, and we would have had that nagging sense of not listening to our inner call to something much bigger.

Big decisions are hard. They don't happen overnight. You need to do your due diligence before taking the plunge. And you need to do the inner work of assessing whether the choices in front of you align with your soul purpose. Looping your intuition into your decision-making is powerful. Trust it to lead you in the right direction.

USING TAROT FOR DECISION-MAKING

Remember when the Magic 8-Ball was all the rage? Whenever you had a question or a decision to make, you could give this black plastic toy a shake and wait for your answer to float to the viewing window. The 8-Ball would reply, "It is certain," or "Signs point to yes," or "Ask again later."

People would spend their whole day shaking this little black ball for every decision. The sad thing was, instead of learning to trust themselves and their inner wisdom, they handed over their free will and sense of empowerment to a little piece of plastic, relying on a toy to tell them what to do.

Tarot is the same. You can ask the Tarot cards, "Should I go to the party tonight?" or "Should I leave my job?" and get a direct yes or no answer. But relying on the cards to tell you what to do leaves no room for your free will or curiosity. And what if you don't like the answer? What if the Tarot told you to leave your job, and then you did but were miserable? ("But the Tarot cards told me to do it!")

The key to using the Tarot in your decision-making is taking ownership of your future and claiming your free will. When you don't take ownership of your future and believe everything is happening *to* you, life can seem like an unpleasant roller-coaster ride. You have little control over your actions or "fate" because you're only working with the hand dealt to you.

But when you believe you can *create* your future, things change. Decision-making becomes a much more conscious process and you discover that you can manifest your goals. That's where Tarot can be a fantastic help. Tarot opens the space to help you think about what's going on and how to make the best choices based on your present circumstances. It reflects *where you are* instead of *what you should do*.

I will say that again because it's very important: **Tarot doesn't show you what you should do. Tarot shows you where you are now so you can make conscious choices about where you are heading.**

Tarot illuminates choices, options, and alternatives that enable—and empower—you to choose the best course of action on your path of self-discovery.

Tarot will never to tell you what to do, nor will the cards decide on your behalf. Instead, Tarot offers information, possibilities, and new insights. You must decide for yourself whether to follow the guidance given. As long as you have your free will, the cards can't "make" you do anything.

WHEN TAROT AND
DECISION-MAKING GO WRONG

· ✴ ✻ ✴ ·

I once received an email from a desperate woman who shared with me that her husband was "addicted" to using the Tarot cards. He had suffered a traumatic event a few months before, and ever since, he felt he needed the Tarot cards to make every decision in his life because he no longer trusted himself.

She told me that one day, he asked the Tarot cards, "Should I go to work today, or take a sick day?" He pulled a card for each option, interpreted their meanings, and said to his wife, "Right, the cards say I should stay home today." And so he did. But unsure of what to do with his day off, he asked, "Should I watch TV or play golf?" It went on like this for the entire day, and then the next day, and the next. His wife was sick of it, as well as concerned for the well-being of her husband.

It was as if her husband could not make a single decision for himself and relied on the Tarot cards as a way of avoiding accountability for his actions.

This dependence is one of the problematic consequences of misusing Tarot for decision-making. You give up your free will to beautifully illustrated pieces of paper. You expect the cards to tell you what you should do, and you expect the cards to be the only answer—without checking in with yourself or seeking other sources of information.

As a result, you disconnect from knowing that you have the power to make choices in your life. You start to believe life happens to you, not because of you, and fall into becoming the victim of "fate." You lose connection with your inner power, and you lose faith in your inner wisdom. Instead, you turn to external sources to show you the way. Take this story as a warning and never forget to use your free will.

HOW TO USE TAROT FOR
EFFECTIVE DECISION-MAKING

· ✳ ✴ ✳ ·

So now that we've established the importance of owning your future and exercising your free will—and looked at what could happen if you don't—it's time to get off the sidelines and see yourself as the *creator* you are! By now, I hope you're warming up to the idea of yourself as a powerful being—but, more than that, I hope you've come to understand that the inner wisdom you hold might not match up with what your ego is telling you.

When you run into a gap between what your intuition is saying to you via the Tarot and what your ego is telling you through the thoughts streaming—or screaming—across your mind, I've got a challenge for you:

Ask the cards about a decision *only once.* Avoid the temptation to keep asking the cards the same question over and over, and choose to see an unexpected response as an opportunity for exploration and discovery. Be curious and open-minded about the possibilities! There may be options that you have not considered before—at least, not consciously. After all, the cards are reflecting your subconscious, rather than your conscious mind.

The tricky part to this is you might feel tempted to charge straight ahead toward the "answer" the cards advise. So stop right there!

Were you just about to hand over your free will to the cards!? #busted.

The information you receive from your reading will be just that—information. It's up to you, the owner of your future, to continue your research. If you're making a business decision, use other business tools and data to support the process. If you're making a choice about a relationship, talk with friends or even your therapist. Don't make the mistake of thinking Tarot is the one and only source of guidance. If you are looking for a "be-all, end-all" source, the voice that carries the most weight? Well, that would be your intuition.

Consult your intuition *before* you consult the Tarot cards. Ask your inner self about the choices available to you and how to make the best decision for your Highest Good, and then use the Tarot cards to go even deeper or uncover aspects of the situation you may not be consciously aware of yet. Go deeper and check in physically and energetically. For each option you are considering, imagine that you have said yes to it. Feel into that choice. Do you expand or contract? Do you feel lighter and brighter or darker and more restricted? Do you have a physical sensation that confirms your choice or shrinks from it?

Intuition is a finely tuned machine. Think of it this way: The conscious mind can only hold between five and nine thoughts or ideas at any given time. It's a little like a Commodore 64 computer from the 1980s and '90s. On the other hand, the subconscious mind is much better at juggling and working through multiple ideas at a time, more like the Acer Predator 21, the most powerful laptop in the world (at a mere $9,000 a pop). People who "go with their gut" are trusting the work their subconscious mind has already done, rather than second-guessing it and relying on their conscious mind's much more limited ability to deal with complex situations.

Remind yourself that the Tarot isn't deciding for you: it doesn't have a mind of its own, and it can't tell you what to do. The final say is ultimately up to you. It may be challenging to have to step up and make a tough decision, but it is your responsibility, and you need to take ownership of the choices you make.

Before we get to our decision-making Tarot spreads, there's one more important point I want to touch upon: asking the right questions.

When you ask the Tarot, "Should I . . . ?" you're giving the Tarot the power to make the decision for you—which we know doesn't work. You are also assuming the Tarot will decide for you. But we all know that it is you who will be making the decision regardless of what the cards say. (Abdicating your free will is, after all, still *your* choice.) So, ask questions that will help you make your decision. For example, "What do I need to know about Option A/B?" or, "What is important to me when making this decision?" Can you feel that subtle, but important, shift in energy?

So promise me something, OK? Use the Tarot as your secret superpower, not your *superhero*, when making conscious decisions. Be the owner of your destiny, and let Tarot be your aide, not your commander.

THE SIMPLE CHOICES
TAROT SPREAD

Decisions come in all shapes and sizes. If you're facing a challenging decision, but one that isn't exactly "high stakes," then a Simple Choices Spread can help.

Elizabeth, a member of the Biddy Tarot community, was picking between two equally fabulous resorts for a romantic trip with her boyfriend. She first asked the Tarot about what they might experience with Resort A and Resort B, drawing the Three of Swords reversed and Four of Cups, respectively. These cards didn't quite give her the clarity she was looking for, so she drew another two cards. For her second reading she asked, "Should we stay at Resort A/B?" (Elizabeth doesn't usually ask yes/no questions of the cards, but this time she felt called to in order to gain more clarity since she was so undecided.)

This time she pulled the Queen of Swords for Resort A, and wondered, "Am I going to be overthinking everything if I go to this destination? Am I going to end up rigid and too focused to really enjoy my vacation?"

For Resort B, she turned over the Ace of Pentacles—her favorite card in her favorite deck! "It was almost an immediate yes for me when I pulled this card," she explained. "It was as if the hand in the card was reaching for mine to bring me along on its journey."

Elizabeth booked the resort straightaway. Reflecting on the reading, she said, "From that point on, I couldn't get any more excited for our vacation! I had truly hoped that our vacation would help us deepen our connection with each other and cultivate our love for one another. And what better sign than the Ace of Pentacles to lead the way!? I am sure to have this card close at hand to really invite its energy throughout our trip and as a token reminder of our decision."

Not only did Elizabeth get clarity from the cards about which resort to choose, she also used the energy of the cards to manifest something beautiful after she had made her choice. In fact, Elizabeth and her partner returned from their trip with a renewed love for one another and a commitment to move in together.

ACTIVITY: THE SIMPLE CHOICES TAROT

· ✳ ·

Start by writing down the decision you're facing. For Elizabeth, it was, "Where should I go for my next holiday?"

Then, list the options you are considering. With an open mind, check in to see if there are any options you have not yet considered, but that could be a possibility.

Now, shuffle your Tarot cards, and for each option, pull a card with the intention that this card will show you what you need to know about that option.

You may not get a clear yes or no, and that's okay. Treat this as intuitive information that you can integrate with what you already know about making this decision. However, if you feel you need more clarity, you might ask, what might I experience if I choose this option? Then draw an extra card for each option.

What if the Tarot showed that none of the options were particularly desirable? Then pull your thinking cap back on and come up with a couple of alternatives and select a card for each of those. Of course, if you are struggling with other options, drawing a card or two can uncover what other choices are available to you.

Finally, if you are still having trouble making a decision, add in a couple of extra questions for the cards to develop some clarity, such as, "What is most important to me?" or "What do I need to know to make a decision?"

THE TWO OPTIONS TAROT SPREAD

I had just started working on the *Everyday Tarot* deck with my publisher and illustrator. I had six Tarot card designs laid out in front of me, each looking beautiful. But I couldn't shake the feeling that something was a little off.

Typically, when a Tarot deck is created, the author and the illustrator work closely together, intertwined in a divine process of "soul transmission." Each person brings a little piece of her soul to the deck as it comes into form, often over a period of one or two years. (Yes, it takes that long!)

This time, though, the process was a little different. Rather than working directly with the illustrator, the publisher served as a go-between. This process works well for book designs, ensuring that an illustrator isn't inundated with feedback. And, luckily for me, my publisher was doing a great job at listening to my feedback and communicating it with the illustrator. But, I still couldn't help but feel like something was out of alignment. This deck wasn't quite feeling like an authentic part of me just yet.

In a moment of panic, I wondered if I should put the brakes on the project altogether. You know, like avoid the problem and pretend like it never happened. (We've all been guilty of that, right?) But in my gut, I knew there had to be a better solution—I just didn't know what it was.

To set my mind at ease, and find guidance toward the best outcome for all involved, I consulted the Tarot cards and laid out my spread.

In the center, I drew two cards for these questions: 1. What is the core issue I'm experiencing right now? 2. What is the deeper spiritual lesson this situation is showing me?

The first card was the Five of Swords—an image of two people walking off in separate directions. To me this was a sign that I felt disconnected from the illustrator, which was leading me to feel disconnected from the deck. The second card was the Three of Cups—three women dancing together and celebrating. Immediately, I knew I needed to create a stronger three-party collaboration between the publisher, the illustrator, and myself, so that I could feel a closer connection to the deck.

Next, I explored each option. On the left-hand side, I drew three cards for Option A—the option of pressing pause on the project. I drew the Page of

Swords reversed (I would be making a reactive, impulsive decision), the Eight of Swords (I would be digging a deeper hole for myself), and the Emperor (while I might be acting "boss" by pausing the project, was this really the energy I wanted to create?).

On the right-hand side, I drew three more cards for Option B—suggesting greater collaboration with the illustrator as we moved into the next phases of the project. I drew the Judgement reversed (my fear of being judged and criticized for the deck), Death (an indication that change was imminent, and we could start afresh), and perhaps the most illuminating card of all, the Page of Cups reversed (a sign that I needed to connect more deeply with my vision for the deck before I started reviewing the individual cards).

You'll notice the meanings I'm sharing are not the kinds you'd find in a book. This is why I love intuitively reading the Tarot cards—because you integrate the images of the cards and your subconscious mind to create deeper connections with what the cards mean for you. With this approach, there is a beautiful extraction of meaning that occurs. You already know, deep down, the best answer or the best path forward, but the Tarot cards help to bring this into your conscious mind. Pretty cool, huh!?

Finally, I drew one more card: What do I need to do/think/feel/be to make the right decision? It was the Sun reversed—a sign that I needed to cultivate a radiant, positive energy around this project and connect with my solar plexus to fully understand my best path forward.

So, I stepped away from my Tarot cards and meditated. I imagined a bright yellow light around my solar plexus chakra, and I experienced a feeling of strength and inner power that would help me make the right decision and go about it in a positive, constructive way. I tuned in to my intuition and asked what would best serve my Highest Good: Option A or Option B? In my heart, I knew that this Tarot deck needed to be birthed into the world and that it would play a very special role, not just in my life, but in the lives of the many people who would use it. I knew I needed to have a more open collaboration with the publisher and artist. But most importantly, I knew I needed to get crystal clear about my vision for the deck.

Next, I started visualizing the Tarot deck: what it meant to me, how it would help others, how it would be received, and what shape and form it might take. I breathed my energy into this deck so that instead of it just being a project that needed to get done, it became a part of me.

Then I reached out to the publisher and asked if we could meet on a call with the illustrator to discuss the greater vision of the deck and make some changes. She happily said yes, and we had the meeting a few days later.

This change made such a difference for me! I could feel the instant connection when I finally got to meet Eleanor, the illustrator, and hear her inspiration for the deck. We shared stories and ideas of where we could take the deck. And together with the publisher, we created this beautiful, combined energy that took the deck to a whole new level. Best of all, I felt like it finally had my energy in it, mixed with the illustrator's and the publisher's—it was that perfect three-way partnership I had seen in the Three of Cups.

Had I not done the Tarot reading, I might have ended up in a very different place. But I trusted my intuition, I made some tough decisions, and we arrived at a solution that worked beautifully for everyone. And now, I couldn't be happier with the Tarot deck and am so proud to put it out into the world.

HOW TO DO IT

· ∗ ✶ ∗ ·

When the stakes are a little higher and the decision you need to make is not as clear-cut as you might like, then this Two Options Tarot Spread is handy for going deeper. You can also extend it to a three or four options spread, depending on how many alternatives are on the table.

Start by writing down the two—or more—options available to you. Think about each possibility and see what comes to you intuitively before you start the reading. What do you already sense to be true about each option? What do you intuitively feel would be the outcome if you were to pursue that option? Which option feels most in alignment with you right now? Write all this down.

Next, shuffle the Tarot cards and do the following spread.

1

What is the core issue
you're experiencing
right now?

3

4

5

What do you
need to know
about Option A?

2

What deeper spiritual
lesson is this situation
showing you?

6

7

8

What do you need
to know about
Option B?

9

What do you need to
do/think/feel/be
to make the right
decision?

Give yourself permission to read the spread intuitively. Traditional Tarot card meanings may come into play, but ultimately, you want to allow your intuition to do the talking. Remember, this is about accessing your inner wisdom, which already has the perfect answer ready for you. Look at the imagery in the cards and see what stands out to you.

And of course, write down your insights and then give yourself some time away from the cards to process what you have discovered and what you feel is your best path forward.

MAKING A DECISION

Oftentimes, the two spreads above are enough to weigh your options and see what's possible with each one. But sometimes, you may still feel stuck about making the right decision and going ahead with it. Use this spread to help you "zoom out" and come to a decision based on what you know.

1		2		3		4

What is at the
root of this
decision?

What new
energy am
I inviting into
my life as I make
this decision?

What's truly
important
to me?

What will help
me make this
decision?

5	6

What might I experience if I
take Option A/Option B?

*(Draw a card for each option
you are considering.)*

7		8

What alternatives
are available to me?

What do I need to
know that I am not
seeing yet?

*(Look at the card on the
bottom of the deck.)*

Again, this Tarot spread is not going to decide for you. But it will help you to uncover your values, opportunities, and potential, so you can land on the decision that is right for you.

DID I MAKE THE RIGHT DECISION?

You've spent weeks and weeks deliberating over a major life decision and finally took the plunge. But now, just days later, you're wondering whether you made the right choice. Does this scenario sound familiar?

Even when you've thought hard about a decision, you can still become anxious about whether you've made the *right* decision. Maybe you're starting to experience the consequences of your decision, and they're not as easy to deal with as you had hoped. Maybe you're beginning to regret the choice you made, or you're feeling guilty about how others have been affected by it.

All this second-guessing can lead you to wonder whether you made the right choice.

But here's the thing: It's not healthy for anyone to dwell on the past. The decision has already been made, and there is no turning back time and opting for something different. Instead, your energy will be better invested if you can focus on how to make your choice work for you, now that you're committed to this path.

That's why I created this seven-card "Did I Make the Right Decision?" Spread to help you do just that.

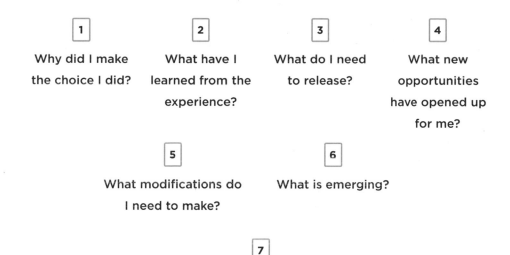

1 Why did I make the choice I did?

2 What have I learned from the experience?

3 What do I need to release?

4 What new opportunities have opened up for me?

5 What modifications do I need to make?

6 What is emerging?

7 Now that I've made this decision, how can I make it work for me?

One of our Biddy Tarot community members, Michelle, recently made the decision to quit her day job and focus on growing her holistic healing business. However, when her family had unrealistic expectations of how she should spend her time now that she was not "employed" and her bank balance was on a steep decline, the doubts started to creep in. So Michelle used the seven-card spread above to find out whether she had made the right decision.

When Michelle laid out the cards and intuitively interpreted their messages, she saw her situation in a new light. "I made this decision because I want to spend more time growing spiritually in my own practice *and* as a practitioner. I *can* have a happy home life, but it will take some work. And I *must* stand my ground and be okay with any opposition that comes my way. I have the strength to do it and it's going to make me a better spiritual coach." She also realized that she needed to stop procrastinating and not allow these external distractions to lead her astray. She knew in her heart that this was her soul path; she just needed to get her ego out of the way and trust in the abundance she knew was coming to her.

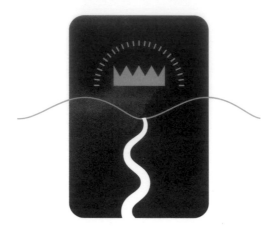

It was the assurance Michelle needed. Despite the challenges that were showing up, she understood she had to persevere and stay true to her purpose and her path. A few months later, she had six new clients and her bank balance was finally on the rise again. Best of all, her husband is now a fierce protector of her work calendar, making sure that any family commitments are scheduled outside of her regular working hours so Michelle can stay focused on her business without interruption.

You are the owner and creator of your future. I will say that again and again and *again*. The decisions you make will shape that future, forging the path of your life with all its twists, turns, bends, hills, and valleys—and that power is yours alone. By tapping into the wisdom of your Higher Self, listening to your intuition, and using the Tarot to add further clarity, you can ensure that the decisions you make stay in alignment with your soul purpose.

And here's the wild thing: there is so much freedom to be found there! Open yourself up to exploring new possibilities you might have never considered. Poke around the ideas that sound scary. And no matter how wild the idea might be—if it resonates, pay attention!

We're going to switch gears a little bit in the next two chapters. It's time to take everything you've learned so far about self-discovery, goals, and decision-making and apply them to two of the most important spheres of your life: your work and your relationships. Are you ready?

Of course you are!

CHAPTER 6

TAROT FOR WORK

WORK. IF YOU'RE LIKE MOST PEOPLE, YOU'LL PROBABLY SEE THAT WORD and groan. Work may be a chore, a bore, and a necessary evil to pay the bills and put food on the table. You work to play. Mondays are depressing, and the weekends come as sweet relief from the daily grind.

But, if you're truly following your heart and listening to your intuition, you'll see that word and your heart will light up with joy and inspiration. Work and play are the same thing when you love what you do.

I want to help you create a work experience and career path that serves your Highest Good, fulfills your soul purpose, and inspires you. This chapter is about creating your own definition of career success—what you do, who you serve, how you grow—and following through with that vision so that work lights you up, every single day. And as always, it's about trusting your intuition—with your Tarot cards as a guide—to lead you to the job and career path that's right for you.

Believe me when I tell you that your intuition can take you down some unexpected paths.

REDEFINING SUCCESS:
MY CAREER JOURNEY

I started my career in my early twenties the way many people do. I studied hard at university and went on to work a full-time job, climbing up the corporate ladder and gaining the approval of my superiors along the way. I aimed to impress others with my professionalism and my tailored suits, making sure that the way I acted at work was in alignment with what was deemed appropriate and professional. I said the right things, connected with the right people, and did the work I was asked to do.

And I did well. I was recognized as "high-performing talent" and given opportunities for ongoing professional development, high-profile projects, and mentoring with some of the best partners in the business. I was scoring goals, and I felt like my career was heading in the right direction.

But as I continued on this path, I started to have a niggling feeling that something wasn't quite in alignment. I enjoyed being a high-flying professional, sure, but was that a true reflection of me?

At this time, I was also reading Tarot on the side and delving deep into spirituality and self-development. I started to understand more about the true self and how important it was to be authentic. Every morning when I walked through the doors to the office, I felt myself putting on my professional self and leaving the more creative, intuitive self at home. I started to feel out of alignment with my integrity—because I wasn't really being me.

Nonetheless, I pushed that feeling to the side and, in 2008, joined a large financial institution, partly to experience a new work environment and partly to find a workplace that supported an important personal goal—starting a family. They had a generous three-month paid maternity leave policy and the opportunity for part-time work. This was when things started to really go downhill.

Within six days of starting, I found myself in the middle of an organizational restructure and my job was put at risk. When I was finally told that I still had a job, I learned it would be very different from what I had been employed to do, and in a different part of the business. I was angry and disappointed because I had not been consulted during the process and was simply told where to go and what to do. I felt my power being stripped away from me. But I persevered because I wanted that paid maternity leave.

Over the following months, I started to notice a number of other worrying aspects of this job and organization. The people who were deemed "successful" by my superiors were highly competitive, in search of approval, status-oriented, and sometimes downright nasty as they played office politics. I found myself getting wrapped up in their drama and negativity but knowing deep down that this wasn't what I truly wanted.

I could feel that light within me beginning to dull and fizzle out. And worse, every day I turned up to work, I couldn't help but look around and think everyone was bananas for being a part of such a broken system filled with yes-people and ongoing resentment.

In 2009, I finally got pregnant with my first daughter and gave birth to her in August. I gladly took the three months' paid, and another six months' unpaid, maternity leave. It was during that time I really started to question whether I was in the right place in my career. I no longer experienced the surge of inspiration and sense of empowerment I had when I was working in consulting. It felt like my power had been completely taken away from me, and that was the worst feeling in the world.

So I started to explore what other options were available, but these were limited, given that I had a young baby and didn't want to work full-time anymore. That's when it clicked: my passion for Tarot could become a business. So while I was on maternity leave, I started to learn more about building and growing an online business.

I eventually went back to my old office again, three days a week, but this time it was different. I was ready to take my power back and make work *work for me*. I listened to marketing podcasts on the way to the office. I used my lunch breaks to advance my business. And I avoided those long coffee chats with colleagues that quickly turned into bitching sessions, so I could get my work done quickly and leave before five p.m. every day. Sure, it was a "Band-Aid" approach, but I was planning for another baby and that paid maternity leave looked mighty good!

By mid-2011, I was on leave again after giving birth to my second daughter. Extending my leave period, we headed to Spain in 2012 for a six-month holiday as a family. It was a huge turning point. I realized that my online Tarot business could make a regular income that would sustain our family—and allow me to do work I love on my own terms. In August 2012, I quit my corporate job and shifted my focus and attention to growing Biddy Tarot into what it is today.

YOUR CAREER, YOUR CHOICE, YOUR SUCCESS

Now I am the creator of my career and my working life. I get to choose what success means to me, how I want to work, and what kind of lifestyle I want to create, not someone else. And best of all, every day I show up at work as my authentic self, fulfilling my potential and my soul purpose—all because I trusted my intuition and relied on my inner wisdom to guide me to be the best version of myself through my career. It is incredibly empowering!

Of course, that doesn't mean you necessarily have to go work for yourself or turn your

passion into your career. The message here is to listen to your intuition and align yourself and your work with what is in your Highest Good.

The more you learn to trust your inner wisdom and intuition, the more you'll realize that *you* get to define for yourself what a successful career and job will look like for you. You decide what work you want to do, how often you work, whom you'll work for or with, and how you want your career to change and develop over time.

The choice is yours and yours alone.

What's my definition of career success? Working for myself and doing work I love, on my own terms. It's creating a scalable company that does not rely on me to operate day by day. It's creating a livelihood that will support my personal goals, including spending time with family, living in a beautiful part of the world, and having the freedom to do what I want. And finally, it's creating work that is in alignment with my Highest Self that enables me to live to my fullest potential.

Your definition of career success might be something totally different, but whatever it is, it should not be a chore or drudgery but something that lights you up!

I asked our Biddy Tarot community what success looked like for them and heard so many different versions. For Jessica, it is working three different jobs—as a part-time barista at the local café, an aspiring artist selling her works at the local market each weekend, and as an energy healer in the evenings. For Rhonda, career success is working as a teacher so she can spend school holidays with her kids. And for Carrie, it's working as a lawyer at a nonprofit that truly aligns with her values around social justice.

Whether you're an employee or self-employed, I want you to recognize your power to choose work that truly inspires and empowers you—on your terms.

So what does that mean to you?

CREATE YOUR CAREER VISION

Let's start with the big picture. When it comes to work and career, what do you want to create? If you could have, do, or be anything you want, what would that look like?

You see, no matter how satisfied or not you are with your career, it's important to begin with what it is you really want and desire. When you envision what you aspire to and bring it into your conscious awareness, then it becomes a possibility. From there, you can take action to turn your vision into reality.

ACTIVITY:
CAREER VISION

For this activity, I encourage you to use both your intuition and your Tarot cards. Start by asking yourself each question and writing down what comes to mind. You may even like to close your eyes and envision what you want to create. Then, draw a Tarot card or two to help you go deeper and uncover any further aspects that you may not have been consciously aware of.

Throughout this activity, keep an open mind and an open heart. Imagine. Don't let fear or doubt creep in and distract you from your dreams. This is big-picture thinking.

Let's dive in . . .

✳ **What does a successful career look like for you?**

✳ **If you could create your dream job, what would it look like?**

✳ **What work would you be doing?**

✳ **What would you be creating?**

✳ **What impact would you have?**

✳   What legacy would you leave?

✳   Whom would you be serving (i.e., your customers)?

✳   Whom would you be working with (i.e., your colleagues and
     partners)?

✳   Would you work for yourself or someone else?

✳   What kind of organization would you work with or create? What
     are its values and how do they align with yours?

✳   What would an ideal workday look like?

✳   What would your work schedule look like?

✳   Where would you be working?

✳   What else would make this dream complete for you?

Revisit your career vision regularly as a reminder of what it is you want to create.

Now, if you're an action-taker like I am, you might be tempted to map out a full plan to help you get from where you are now to where you want to be within a certain time frame. If that feels good to you, go ahead and do it—using your cards to guide you through the process. But, there's something else I want you to know: the simple task of envisioning what you want and bringing it into your conscious awareness is a big part of the action process. You are planting a seed for what is possible. So don't feel you have to hurry into action—some of that action will come through the choices you make from this moment forward.

CAREER ALIGNMENT CHECK-IN

I was sitting in a meeting room on the thirty-second floor of an office building, overlooking the Melbourne cityscape. Across from me was the managing director of a large consulting firm and two other partners. I was sweating bullets. It was my dream to work for a firm like this one, and I wanted the job so badly. After some small talk about the weather and the view, the managing director turned to me and looked me directly in the eyes, asking, "So, Brigit. Where do you see yourself in five years?" Inside I was freaking out—I had no five-year career plan! I was twenty-three years old! So I calmly responded, "It doesn't really matter, so long as I am happy." He paused for a moment with a quizzical look on his face. "You mean you don't want to be a general manager or a partner in a business?" he asked. To which I responded, "Well I might, but how do I know that now? Isn't it better to seek happiness, whatever that might be?" He seemed astounded that I was more driven by a desire to be happy than to follow a predetermined career path. Nonetheless, I think he was secretly impressed with my answer because I got the job and went on to become a top employee in the company!

Here's the thing: When you are in full alignment with who you really are and what you really want, you understand the value of the present moment and you are in tune with where you are now. You may have a vision for the future, but what matters is how you feel right now and whether what you are doing is in alignment with what feels right for you in the present.

So that's why I created this Career Alignment Check-In: to help you assess where you are and how you can bring your career into better alignment with your true self. This allows for the space to listen deeply to whether you are in the right place or if you need a change and a career transition is imminent (more on that later).

ACTIVITY:
CAREER ALIGNMENT CHECK-IN
· * ✳ * ·

Pull out your favorite Tarot deck and your notebook. Take a moment to ground yourself with a few deep breaths and meditation. We're about to get into some deep stuff.

Go through each question or choose the questions that are most relevant to you right now, and first reflect using your intuition and inner wisdom. Write down your insights in your notebook. Then, pull a Tarot card for each question to help you go deeper and access your subconscious mind.

Look for relationships between the questions. For example, is there a gap between how you feel about your career now and what a successful career looks like for you? Find where you may be out of alignment and discover what steps you can take to bring a greater sense of fulfillment in your career.

1	2	3	4
How do I feel about my career right now?	What is working well for me?	What is not working well for me?	What impact is my work having on others?

5	6	7	8
What impact is my work having on me?	What does a successful, healthy career look like for me?	What do I want to achieve in my career that I don't have now?	How can I balance my work aspirations with my personal aspirations?

9

Which aspects
of my gifts or
talents do I most
want to use in
my work?

10

Which new skills
do I most want
to develop
and learn?

11

What aspects
of my career do
I want to
do *more*?

12

What aspects of
my career do I
want to do *less*?

13

What resources
(*people, organi-
zations, etc.*)
are available
to me to
increase my
career success?

14

What new
values are
emerging when
it comes to
my career?

15

What new career
opportunities
are calling
to me?

16 +

What are my
next steps
toward aligning
my current
career with my
aspirations?

(*Draw up to
three cards.*)

FIND YOUR DREAM JOB

Most of us want to do work that is meaningful, purposeful, and aligns with our values. Yet, in reality, the majority of people are disengaged from their work and dissatisfied with their work situation, according to the Gallup organizational research firm.

If you feel your job is sucking your soul right out of you, you have a choice: you can choose to stay where you are and do nothing, putting up with a job that doesn't serve your deeper needs, or you can actively seek out new opportunities that are more in keeping with your values and desires. To find out what is truly in alignment, it's essential you go within by connecting with your inner wisdom and your Tarot cards to see the bigger picture.

So how do you do that? It comes down to getting clear on what you want, creating an action plan, and consciously choosing the opportunities that are right for you.

1) GET CLEAR ABOUT YOUR DREAM JOB

· ✳ ✴ ✳ ·

If you're unhappy in your current job but don't put in the work to figure out why and what you want instead, it's likely you will find yourself in an equally dissatisfying job if you make a move. That's why it's important to get clear about what you truly desire in your next job before you begin your job search.

I recommend first starting with the Career Vision activity earlier in this chapter and then zoom in with the following questions, which will help you focus on what you want when it comes to your next job.

ACTIVITY

For each question below, first check in with your intuition and write what comes to mind. Then draw a Tarot card for each question to go deeper.

✳ **What is the core reason for me wanting to leave my current job?**

✳ **What do I dislike about my current job?**

✳ **What do I most desire in my next job?**

✳ **What do I most desire from my next employer?** *(e.g., pay, flexibility, meaning, respect, etc.)*

✳ **What do I most desire in my next work environment?** *(e.g., people and culture)*

✳ **What is in alignment with my definition of career success?**

✳ **What skills and talents do I have to offer?**

⁕ How can I best use my strengths and talents in my next job?

⁕ What impact do I want to have in my next job?

⁕ How will I know when I have found the right job?

Later, when you are weighing up your options and choosing the right job for you, reflect on what you have discovered here and make sure there is a fit with what you truly desire.

2) CREATE YOUR DREAM JOB SEARCH PLAN

· ⁕ ✱ ⁕ ·

Now that you know what your dream job looks like, it's time to figure out how to make that dream a reality.

Your Tarot cards—and your common sense—can help you to map out a job search plan. Applying for advertised jobs will only take you so far. According to LinkedIn, eighty percent of jobs are found through networking, *not* via a job ad. So think creatively about how you can actively find the job opportunities that are right for you.

ACTIVITY

Grab your Tarot cards, a pen, and paper.

First, ask your Higher Self, "What steps can I take to find my dream job?" Write down every idea that comes to mind, thinking about who can help you, where you can find the right job, and how you can seek it out. Then, when you've exhausted your ideas, shuffle your Tarot deck and pull three cards. What new information do these cards give you? Draw on your intuitive interpretation of the cards.

Be on the lookout for Tarot cards that may indicate how to go about finding a job, such as using a recruitment agency, online job search, personal networks, etc. For example, the Three of Cups or the Queen of Wands emphasizes the importance of social networking. The Hierophant or Three of Pentacles points to being a part of a professional association. The Three of Wands suggests online job searching with a possibility of working overseas.

And the Emperor may indicate a recruitment agency. Go with your gut and see where your intuition leads you.

Now, go back through your list, and circle the actions you commit to take in your dream job search and enter them in your calendar or to-do list to make sure they happen.

Finally, think about what energy will be most helpful in your job search and go through your Tarot deck to consciously select one card that rep-

resents that energy. For example, you might choose the Six of Wands for confidence or the Fool for a completely new job experience or even the King of Swords for a managerial position towards which you aspire. Carry this card with you to help you manifest that energy and use it to your advantage during your job search.

And as you take action, continually check in with your intuition to make sure you're still on the right track.

3) CONSCIOUSLY CHOOSE THE JOB THAT'S RIGHT FOR YOU

· ✳ ✶ ✳ ·

If you've been taking action to find your dream job, then it is likely you are starting to see new opportunities opening up for you. As they do, you will need to work out whether each one is the right fit for you or not.

Be careful—this is where we can sometimes be led astray. In the excite-ment of being invited to an interview or offered a job, we think we need to do everything to please and impress our prospective employers. But really, it's a two-way process. Your prospective employer is checking you out for "fit," and you need to do the same for them. It's all part of reclaiming your inner power and acknowledging that you can make conscious choices about your work and how you spend your time and energy.

HOW TO ASSESS NEW OPPORTUNITIES

First, revisit what you discovered when you clarified what you want in a dream job. Keep this top of mind as you evaluate whether new opportunities are right for you.

Then, as new opportunities arise, run each one through the following tests to see if it really is your dream job.

Ask the Tarot and your Higher Self:

| What might I experience if I accept this opportunity? | How might I experience the job? | How might I experience the organization? | How might I experience the work environment? |

Now, compare these insights with what you desire in your dream job. To what extent is there alignment between this job and your values?

Next, ask the Tarot and your Higher Self:

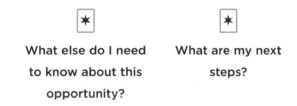

| What else do I need to know about this opportunity? | What are my next steps? |

By this stage, you'll probably already have a sense of whether or not this is the right opportunity for you. However, if you're still feeling indecisive or weighing a number of positive options, then use any of the techniques from chapter 5 to support your decision-making.

Here's my invitation to you. Decide now that you will no longer settle for meaningless, uninspiring work. Envision your dream job and actively design a working life that aligns your purpose with your paycheck.

MAKING A CAREER TRANSITION

There may come a time on your career path when you no longer feel connected to the work. You may feel exhausted, burnt out, disenchanted, or resentful. You don't want to just show up and get paid, but to make a difference and have an impact. Could it be that you're hearing a call to make a change—a *big* change—in your career direction?

For me, it happened in my early thirties when I decided to walk away from my corporate life to follow my passion and build my own business. For Biddy Tarot community member Laura, it was in her forties as she started to realize that while she was talented at her job as a web developer, what she really wanted to do was heal others with Reiki and crystals. And for Katie, after ten years of working as a teacher, she decided to change direction and enrolled in a graphic design course.

Career transitions are hard, and they are scary. Work is a source of income, and that means the possibility of change can draw out your survival needs in full effect. *I can't give up this money and security,* your ego might scream. But your intuition might be telling you something else.

The key is in trusting yourself, your intuition, and your inner guidance to light the way. Of course, you need to have some common sense too and make sure that you are able to sustain your lifestyle while transitioning from one career to the next. I encourage you to spend a lot of time gathering information and assessing your options—even the ones you can't see yet.

PHASE 1:
AWARENESS

Often awareness of a career change emerges when we go through any personal development—a spiritual awakening, a deeper understanding of our soul purpose, or a significant life event that forces us to reevaluate our priorities and values. (See chapter 3 for ideas on how to use Tarot to help you in your personal development process.)

If you're reading this part of the book, no doubt you are experiencing an awareness that there is something more for you when it comes to career. The awareness is often quite clear, but what might not be clear is what you are being called *to*.

ACTIVITY

Pull out your cards and ask the Tarot:

1	2	3	4
In what ways does my current career path serve me?	In what ways does my current career path hinder me?	To what extent is my current career in alignment with my soul purpose?	What new possibilities are emerging for me?

Remember to use both your Tarot cards *and* your intuition. For example, the Knight of Pentacles might show you that your career path gives you a sense of structure and forward movement, while your intuition might remind you that you enjoy having interactions and conversations with your colleagues. These are all relevant pieces of information that will help you decide whether a career transition is right for you.

PHASE 2:
DISCOVERY

Once you've heard the call to pursue something new in your career, the next step is discovery—identifying your current and emerging talents and understanding how you can channel these into a new career path that will bring you a deeper sense of purpose.

You may already have a sense of how you want to express your skills and talents in a new career. Or, if you're like most people, you may need to create space to step into the "void" and explore how you want to transform yourself.

My friends the Merrymaker Sisters experienced this recently. They knew that their current business direction was not going to keep serving them into the future. Still, they felt frustrated because they wanted the discovery phase to be done and dusted within just a few days or weeks. They weren't used to sitting in the pregnant pause of discovery.

I encouraged them to surrender to the process and to be fully present in the nothingness, holding space for whatever might emerge. After a few months, they finally came up with an amazing business idea, filled with energy and excitement for the future—all because they trusted this void and allowed it to open up new possibilities for them.

ACTIVITY

To help you get started with the discovery phase, ask the Tarot *and* your intuition:

1	2	3	4
What is my soul purpose?	How might my soul purpose align with my career?	What are my gifts and talents?	How can I integrate these gifts and talents in my career?

5	6	7	8 +
How can I serve others?	What might a fulfilling, purpose-driven career look like for me?	What new career opportunities are emerging for me?	What three things could I try? (Draw three cards.)

It's okay to leave a little space for "magic" here. You don't have to have all the answers about what the perfect soul-aligned career would be. But start to get some ideas of what it could look like. It will evolve and change over time. The discovery phase is simply about creating a vision of what's possible.

Plant those seeds. Try a few things out. Take a few classes before you go all-in. And see where it takes you. Treat everything as an experiment to discover what you do and don't like. You can't lose!

PHASE 3:
COMMITMENT
· ✳ ✳ ·

The discovery phase is *huge*. It can last a few weeks, a few months, or even a few years. But at some point, there will come a time when you are finally ready to make a decision and commit to your career transition.

The commitment phase is when you weigh all of your options, check for alignment to your personal values, and then make the decision about which path you'll take.

In chapter 5, you discovered how to make intuitively led decisions using Tarot. You may find some of those techniques helpful as you take ownership of your career transition.

TAROT ACTIVITY

Ask the Tarot—and your intuition—the following questions to check in if you are ready to move ahead with your envisioned career transition.

1	2	3	4
What's the impact of staying in my current career?	What's holding me back from making a career transition?	How can I let that go?	What's the impact of leaving my current career?

5	6	7	8
What's possible if I start a career transition?	What do I need to do to make this a successful career transition?	What other alternatives are available to me?	What is the deeper lesson for me as I make this decision?

PHASE 4:
INTENTION
· * ✦ * ·

Now that you have committed to making a career transition, it's time to set your intentions and map out your transition. This is all about figuring out what it's going to take to make this career change real.

Start with an audit of your current skills and resources, and what you'll need to develop to step into the new career path you're considering. Do you need to take a course, get new qualifications, create new networks, or seek out a mentor?

Keep it real with an idea of what you may need to sacrifice as you pursue your new career. I hate to break it to you, but dream careers don't happen overnight. You're going to have to let a few things go by the wayside while you pursue your next move. For example, you may need to put in long hours, study while you work your full-time job, or take a significant cut to your regular income. When I was growing Biddy Tarot and exploring whether it had the potential to become a business, I had to sacrifice a lot! There were late-night hustles after hours of soothing my crying baby and weekends filled with work.

Finally, start to map out your immediate next steps. What do you need to do to move toward your new career path?

TAROT ACTIVITY

Here are five questions to help get you started:

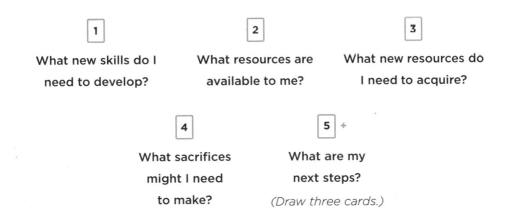

1	2	3
What new skills do I need to develop?	What resources are available to me?	What new resources do I need to acquire?

4	5 +
What sacrifices might I need to make?	What are my next steps? (Draw three cards.)

PHASE 5:
ACTION

You've set the intention for your career transition. The next step is to take action.

Start small. What are the incremental changes you can make that will bring you closer to your career goals? Each little action you take will give you information and feedback about whether you're heading in the right direction. And if you find you're not, then you can adjust your course.

TAROT ACTIVITY

As you take action toward your new career path, use your Tarot cards to check in regularly. Each action leads to the next, so you want to make sure that you're heading in the right direction, in alignment with your soul purpose and values, and clear on the next step in front of you.

Every week, or every month, ask the Tarot:

How am I tracking?   **What's my next step?**

Tarot works beautifully with understanding career direction and making career transitions. It is the bridge between what you think is the right path and what you know on a deeper level to be the right path.

You can go beyond what you think is expected of you or from parents screaming, "What about your university education?!" or "Why are you walking away from a six-figure job?!" and get deeper into your true calling.

CHAPTER 7

TAROT FOR
LOVE +
RELATIONSHIPS

WE ALL DESIRE CONNECTION. WE SEEK TO BE SEEN, HEARD, AND understood by others. We yearn to love and be loved. It makes perfect sense, then, that the health of your relationships is one of the most influential factors in your day-to-day happiness.

Now, before we go any further, I want to address the problematic idea of finding "the one."

I believe that striving to find "the one" person you're meant to be with will sign you up for a lot of unnecessary heartaches. "The one" assumes that there is only one person out there, but there are so many great people with whom you could connect deeply. What happens if you don't find "the one"? How many great people might you brush off because you're busy looking for that single, solitary person? Finally, I think that mindset presumes that once you have found "the one," the hard work is over and you will be together happily forever after, but we know that good relationships take effort, work, and commitment.

If there is any single person who holds the keys to your love and happiness, it's *you*. How we relate to the concept of love is often tied to our self-worth—and it all starts with loving yourself unconditionally.

THE ETHICS OF RELATIONSHIP READINGS

When consulting the Tarot about relationships, it can be very tempting to start asking questions like, "How does he feel about me?" "Is she cheating on me?" or "Is he *really* in love with his new girlfriend or is he still dreaming about me and wishing I'll come back to him?"

It can seem as though these little cards can turn into lie detectors or all-telling truth serums. But trust me, you don't want to go there.

The problem with asking the Tarot these kinds of questions is that you start to shift the focus from yourself to another person, and in so doing you also move your source of power and control from yourself to someone else.

You see, when you ask the Tarot cards about yourself, you can take action to manifest the outcomes you want. But when you ask the Tarot cards about someone else, you might get an answer, but you can't do anything about it. Don't hand over your sense of control over your future! Keep the focus of the reading on yourself and the actions you can take in the situation.

For example, Beth wanted to know if her new love interest was as "head over heels" for her as she was for him. So, she pulled a card and got the Four of Cups, a sign that he wasn't into her. Now, Beth could have spent the rest of the day crying in her bathroom, gutted that her dreams of marrying this guy had been crushed to smithereens. Instead, she held on to her inner power and brought her focus back to herself: "Right, if he's not into me, I should let him go and find someone who is." Then she drew another card to figure out who would be a good fit for her.

It all comes down to what you do with information. You can get depressed if it's not what you want to hear, or you can take ownership of the situation and make the changes necessary to manifest your goals and dreams. Beth chose to take control, and a few months later, she met her long-term partner. Had she stuck with the first guy, she might have missed the opportunity.

Using the Tarot cards to figure out someone else's feelings can also be inaccurate. When you ask how someone else feels about you, you might think it's like becoming a psychic spy and reading their mind. But what happens is that you interpret their feelings based on what you feel. Rather than asking, "How does so-and-so feel about me?" you're asking, "How do I think so-and-so feels about me?" See the difference?

My advice is to start with *you*. Loving yourself is the key to attracting the love you want.

IT ALL STARTS WITH SELF-LOVE

Love, in any form, starts with love for yourself.

When you love yourself unconditionally, you fully accept and appreciate who you are, and you deeply respect and honor the truest version of yourself. You welcome a life of happiness and fundamentally believe you deserve to feel good about yourself. And when you come from this place of self-love, self-acceptance, and self-respect, you will have more fulfilling, loving relationships with others.

Here's the thing: if you don't love yourself, you'll end up projecting your lack of love onto others, becoming clingy and attached, attracting the wrong kinds of relationships to you, or worse, ending up in harmful situations.

For Alejandra, her lack of self-love resulted in her attracting an alcoholic boyfriend and a series of bosses who treated her poorly within the workplace. For Cheryl, she recently became aware that when she does not value herself, others take advantage of her and she feels used and hurt. And as for Megan, she says, "Before I understood what self-love was, I was constantly giving to others and not myself. I said yes, even if I didn't want to, and found myself feeling exhausted and burnt out."

On the flip side, if you love yourself, you will attract and keep only the most fulfilling relationships that serve your Highest Good, and be able to completely give and receive love without attachment or expectation.

So before you seek out your Prince Charming or tie the knot with your lifetime love, make sure you've filled your cup with all that beautiful love juice for yourself first. To find fulfillment in your life and relationships, you have to find the love within you and give it to yourself. No other person, material possession, or accomplishment can do it. It's entirely up to *you*.

TAROT CARDS FOR SELF-LOVE

Start the self-love journey by using the Tarot cards as visual reminders or affirmations of what you want to create with unconditional love. Go through your deck and choose one card that represents what self-love means to you. Following are five suggestions to help get you started.

STAR

The Star is the healer card of the Tarot deck. If you need to restore your faith in yourself and the Universe, hold on to this card. This is also about accessing your true self and being authentic. It is about accepting who you are in your wholeness.

Self-Love Affirmation: *I believe in myself.*

NINE OF PENTACLES

The Nine of Pentacles resembles a strong, independent woman who has both financial and spiritual wealth. She is confident in her continuous flow of abundance, and she's not afraid to spend a little cash on her personal well-being. Bring on the 24-karat gold facial, please!

Self-Love Affirmation: *I deserve love and abundance.*

EMPRESS

The Empress is your booty-licious goddess (hello, Beyoncé!) who loves her curvy body and radiates beauty and sensuality. Her love is abundant, not just for herself but others too, and she knows the value of nurturing and caring.

Self-Love Affirmation: *I love my body.*

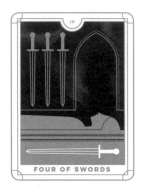

FOUR OF SWORDS

Self-love often means self-care. If you're due for a little downtime, the Four of Swords is your friend. Sign up for that vegan yoga retreat in the tropical rainforest, I say!

Self-Love Affirmation: *I give myself permission to rest and restore my energy.*

QUEEN OF CUPS

If you spend most of your days looking after others—friends, lovers, kids, family—the Queen of Cups calls you back to looking after yourself with love and care.

Self-Love Affirmation: *I love and nurture myself.*

Once you have chosen your self-love card, have a conversation with the figure in the card, or if that feels dorky, write it down in your journal. What advice would they give you about loving yourself unconditionally? What words of encouragement do they have for you? If they were in your shoes, what would they do?

Then, place the card on your altar or somewhere a little more practical like your handbag, desk, bedside table, or bathroom. Have it as a visual reminder of what self-love means to you every day. And repeat the Self-Love Affirmation three times daily, speaking the words out loud and proud.

Do this for at least twenty-one days to allow your chosen card's energy to positively influence your self-love and self-respect. Then check in with yourself and how you feel about self-love now. You can use free-flow writing or meditation if you want to get deep. I'm going to bet you're filled with so much good juju, you'll be glowing!

SELF-LOVE TAROT SPREAD

· ✳ ✦ ✳ ·

If you're having one of those premenstrual days, feeling down about yourself, or want to dig deeper into creating more love for yourself, try out this Self-Love Tarot Spread to pick up your spirits again.

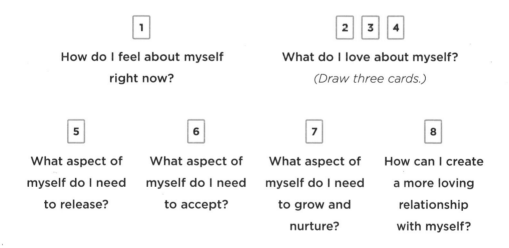

How do I feel about myself right now?

What do I love about myself?
(Draw three cards.)

What aspect of myself do I need to release?

What aspect of myself do I need to accept?

What aspect of myself do I need to grow and nurture?

How can I create a more loving relationship with myself?

Add another layer of insight to the reading by journaling your personal responses to each question, using the Tarot cards to help you go deeper.

DAILY SELF-LOVE RITUAL

· * ✦ * ·

If you want to give your self-love an extra boost, try out this daily self-love ritual. It's perfect for reaffirming all the beautiful parts of yourself and why you are ever so deeply in love with yourself.

Every day, for at least seven days, ask the Tarot, "What do I most love about myself?" Draw a card, then spend ten minutes journaling about what you love and appreciate about yourself based on this card. Start each sentence with "I love that I . . ."

And hey, if it feels like a total bragfest, don't worry—it totally is! I give you my loving permission to brag about how awesome you are until the cows come home.

As an example, let's say you draw an Ace of Wands. Your journal entry might say something like this:

I love that I am inspired by new ideas. I love that I am filled with passion and inspiration. I love that I can see the best in others and that I can match up their skills and passions to offer them a new possibility. I love that I can see the world through inspired eyes, that I see potential all around me.

I dare you not to feel good after practicing this kind of affirmation! Remember this: you don't attract what you *want*, you attract what you *are*—and that's one of the infinite reasons why feeling uplifted, powerful, and "high-vibe" is essential!

HOW TO ATTRACT TRUE LOVE

"I've found him! I've finally found 'the one'!" My friend Jemma was squealing on the other end of the phone like an excited kid even though she's in her mid-thirties.

Only two years ago, she had been sobbing as she packed her boxes, selling her home and reluctantly leaving behind her then-husband. She was in tears, wondering if she would ever find love and whether she could trust someone again.

She set up a profile on the online dating app Tinder, hopeful that she might attract her dream guy. She was determined not to be that bitter, resentful divorced woman, and instead put herself out there, ready to find love again.

But the first few months of dating were a disaster. There was the guy who went all "fifty shades of grey" on their first date—and not in a good, sexy way. And the guy who was so addicted to Tinder that he sat through their entire dinner together scrolling for the next match. And the guy who seemed super-sweet with his new puppy, but two weeks later was sending the pup back to the shop because it was too much work. "What kind of monster returns a puppy!?" Jemma asked me, throwing her hands in the air in exasperation.

It was back to the drawing board—literally. Keen to put love on a fast track to success, Jemma created a vision board for the kind of relationship she wanted to create. She found pictures of people who were feeling what she wanted to feel: people laughing, having a good time, and enjoying life together. She clipped out photos of famous entrepreneurial couples—since Jemma is an entrepreneur herself—in dreamy relationships. And she found pictures of happy families with beautiful kids and sexy husbands, including one of a handsome man and two blonde children.

As she was creating this beautiful vision board, she started to notice a few doubts creeping in. "Who's going to want to date a divorced thirty-year-old? What if all the good ones are taken? Am I going to have to settle for one of these oddballs from Tinder?" But instead of getting bogged down by these limiting beliefs, Jemma switched her focus to a powerful visualization she had found online. She imagined herself as her dream partner, looking through his eyes and looking at her, filled with love. She visualized what he would feel—respect, love, and adoration. And through this process, her self-love went through the roof, and she fundamentally believed that she was lovable once again. "Right!" she said. "I'm ready to find love! Bring it on!"

Not having had a great experience on Tinder, Jemma decided she needed to change her strategy: no more Tinder and no more dating people she didn't know. She opened the Tinder app on her phone, ready to delete her profile, but something stopped her in her tracks. There on her phone was a photo of a handsome man—someone she had worked with before, someone she knew.

She "swiped right" and within a few days, they were going on their first date (on the same day as her wedding anniversary with her ex-husband).

Now, two years later, they're happily living together. And here's the funny thing: Jemma's manifesting powers were even more switched on than she realized. Remember that picture of a handsome man with two blonde kids? Her intention was that she would attract the love of her life and have two beautiful kids together. Well, it almost turned out that way—except that he already came with kids in tow!

FIVE STEPS TO ATTRACTING LOVE

· * ✳ * ·

I wish I could tell you that with a wave of my magic wand I could make your romantic dreams come true, but you'd know I'd be lying. Attracting meaningful love into your life takes work.

In fact, much of the work happens even before you lay eyes on your new dreamy man or woman. It's all about laying the foundations and doing the groundwork to attract not just any relationship but the *right* relationship into your life. It's about getting clear about what and whom you want to attract, removing any blocks or limiting beliefs about love, and opening yourself up to give and receive love unconditionally.

Here are the five steps to finding your soul mate—and how the Tarot can help you:

1. **Define what and whom you want to attract.**

2. **Clear any limiting beliefs or blocks about love.**

3. **Be your best self.**

4. **Show up and take action.**

5. **Be open to love and trust the process.**

Let's look a little deeper into each step.

1) DEFINE WHAT AND WHOM YOU WANT TO ATTRACT

Any good manifesting project starts with getting clear about what it is you want to manifest. Thinking about your ideal relationship and partner, what do you want to attract and grow?

Focus on what you would like to feel and experience, rather than getting into the nitty-gritty, he-must-look-like-Ryan-Gosling details.

If you find yourself thinking about all the things you don't want, be sure to change those over to what you do want. If you focus only on the negatives, guess what you'll attract? Most people keep attracting poor partners, not because of lack of focus, but because they put all their energy into what they don't want!

Remember what you define must excite the hell out of you. You want to be able to read your list of ideal relationship/partner attributes and be jumping out of your skin to create that in your life.

To help you with this, ask the Tarot and your intuition the following questions:

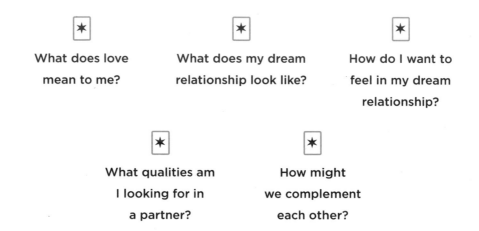

What does love
mean to me?

What does my dream
relationship look like?

How do I want to
feel in my dream
relationship?

What qualities am
I looking for in
a partner?

How might
we complement
each other?

For each question, draw a Tarot card and spend at least ten minutes writing your responses in your journal. Use the Tarot card as an initial prompt and then integrate what your heart is calling you toward.

Your answers will help you create a map of your desires and show you what energies to cultivate in your life. This is the cornerstone of attracting great love.

And if you feel called as Jemma did, create a vision board with images of the type of relationship and partner you would like to attract. Focus on how you want to feel, rather than what you want him or her to look like. (You can't fill your vision board with *just* Ryan Gosling pictures, okay?!)

2) CLEAR ANY LIMITING BELIEFS OR BLOCKS ABOUT LOVE

"I'm not good enough for a loving relationship."

"I'm too fat/ugly/old to attract a decent partner."

"All the good ones are taken."

"I've been hurt in the past. I can never love openly again."

"I have to get married before thirty-five, otherwise I'll never have kids."

Have you ever caught yourself saying one or more of these things? If so, you've got to clear those blocks, baby!

To discover your blocks to love, ask yourself, "What makes me doubt that I can have a loving relationship?" The answer will show you precisely what beliefs you need to release to transform your experience in love.

Write your responses in your journal. Then, ask your Tarot cards for some extra insight and take note.

Next, ask the Tarot, "How can I release these limiting beliefs?"

If you wish to go deeper into this process of identifying and releasing your limiting beliefs around love, I encourage you to revisit the exercises we discussed in chapter 3.

3) BE YOUR BEST SELF

If you want to attract someone awesome, then you need to be awesome. And you know where it starts, right? Self-love, baby!

When you unconditionally love and respect yourself, you will attract others who love and respect you, and you will repel or expel those who do not.

My friend Jemma did this when she envisioned looking through her dream partner's eyes back at herself and feeling all the feelings she wanted her dream partner to experience about her. She couldn't help but sense the self-love welling up and filling her soul.

And it's when you're in this beautiful place that love begins to flow. So, pull out those Tarot cards and ask the following:

| What is the very best version of myself? | How can I share the best version of myself with others? | What aspects of myself do I need to grow to attract love? | What aspects of myself do I need to release to attract love? |

As always, use the Tarot cards as a journaling prompt, then integrate your insights with your innermost thoughts. I want you getting to the place where you are bursting with love and affection for yourself and super-clear about why you are awesome and how you can radiate your awesomeness out into the world to attract your perfect relationship.

4) SHOW UP AND TAKE ACTION

It's one thing to dream of your ideal relationship. But if you're not showing up where you're likely to find your perfect partner, your chances of meeting them are low.

The most practical way to "show up" is to leave your house and get out into the world. Hang out at your local café, join clubs, take group classes, go to the beach, work with other people you like, take a trip. Do something fun!

And here's a pro tip—trust your intuition and follow the signs. Jason, a friend of mine, was working at his local café when he overheard a group of people talking about a yoga retreat upstate. He wasn't into yoga, so he didn't think much of it. But the next day, he was catching up with a friend who happened to mention she was going to this yoga retreat and he should come. Well, he usually would have said, "No way—that's not my thing!" but he knew to pay attention to the signs and, because he'd heard those people talking about the retreat the day before, he knew it meant something. What was also interesting was that he was scheduled to travel for work at the time of the retreat, but at the last minute, the trip got canceled. It was a big, fat *yes* from the Universe! So he went along, and within a day he'd met a beautiful yogini named Julia and two years later they are happily married!

So the simple advice is to get out there and show up. And if you need a little shove from the Universe, take your Tarot cards and ask, "What do I need to do to find and attract love?" Perhaps the Three of Cups will entice you to go dancing with your girlfriends, or the Knight of Cups will show you a desert oasis and an exotic trip to Morocco? Trust the signs and go with it.

5) BE OPEN TO LOVE AND TRUST THE PROCESS

You've created your vision of your ideal relationship, let go of any limiting beliefs, aligned with your best self, and started taking action. Now what?

Here is the tricky part, my friend: you need to let go and trust the process.

When you hold too firmly to the need to find a partner, you create fear and anxiety for yourself. Questions like "When will I meet him?" and "How long until I find love?" feed into this fear. But you can't attract love from fear. You can't attract love when you're trying to control the process. You can only attract love from love. That's why you have to trust, let go, and allow the process to unfold.

To support you in trusting the Universe and your intuition to guide you toward the right opportunities, you may want to draw a Tarot card at the start of each week, asking, "What is unfolding for me as I attract true love?" It's essential that you create your sacred space and center your mind before pulling this card so that you have a clear reading—and not one of those where you're desperately trying to find Prince Charming in the Ten of Swords!

As we've discussed, it's not enough to just look for insight from your inner wisdom via the Tarot. You've got to work it! In the case of love and relationships, that means mindfully and intentionally drawing the insight you get from the cards out into your reality. Whether that means pampering yourself when you recognize a need for self-care or biting your tongue when your partner is airing an issue that you feel aggrieved by, be conscious of your opportunities to put your newfound wisdom into practice.

This holds especially true when you're dating.

CONSCIOUS DATING

When I was single, I loved dating. I loved the thrill of the chase and using my feminine energy to seduce and charm potential love interests. On any given weekend, my girlfriends and I would get dressed up and go out on the town, excited about the possibility of meeting new people. We'd dance all night long and flirt with the boys, and if it was a good night, we might swap numbers with a hunky guy. It was super-fun and filled me with a beautiful, powerful energy that affirmed I was lovable, sexy, and radiant.

Sometimes though, it would go too far, and I found myself feeling like I had lost my power rather than gaining it. I would give too much of myself or would try to impress others at the cost of my self-love and respect.

Despite the ups and the downs, being actively single was one the most enlightening times of my life. I came to a point where I realized that every person I met showed me something new about myself. For example, one guy was madly in love with me, and while I enjoyed his company, I wasn't attracted to him. He showed me that it was okay to say no. Another guy was four years my junior—quite a gap in your early twenties—and showed me how to be a little less serious and have some spontaneous fun.

The more self-aware you can be when you are dating, the more you learn. You figure out what kinds of relationships are right for you and how you want to act in those relationships. And, yes, the Tarot can help you dive deeper into those lessons, too.

See your dating life as a tremendous opportunity to expand your being on a grand scale. Treat every new love interest as a spiritual guide, here to show you something about yourself and open you up to your heart and how you want to love and be loved.

HOW TO HAVE A GREAT DATE EVERY SINGLE TIME

· * ✸ * ·

If you have a romantic rendezvous coming up and want a little intuitive insight, try this Hot Date Tarot Spread:

1	2
What is my intention for the date?	What is his/her intention for the date?

3	4
What might I experience during the date?	Where might this date lead?

5	6
What is my karmic connection with this person?	How can I make the most of this experience?

Quick tip: If the cards suggest the date will be a total disaster, avoid the temptation to cancel your plans. Go in with an open mind and be ready to accept the lesson offered to you. Pay attention to those last two cards to discover how to go into this date consciously.

THE "IS THIS RELATIONSHIP GOING ANYWHERE?" SPREAD

In your love journey, you are going to meet many potential interests. Some may be a bit of noncommittal fun. Others may woo you at the start, but quickly show themselves as not the right fit. And others may develop into the most meaningful, long-term relationships in your life. The key is to know when a new relationship is heading in the right direction—and when it is not. (There's nothing worse than trying to woo someone over when they're just not that into you.)

Here's a Tarot spread I've created to help you get to the bottom of whether the relationship is going anywhere or not.

1	2	3	4
How are you in the relationship with your partner?	What are your intentions for the relationship?	How is your partner in the relationship with you?	What are your partner's intentions for the relationship?

5	6	7
What is the current state of the relationship?	What is working well in the relationship?	What isn't working well?

8	9	10	11
Where is the relationship heading?	What is the long-term potential of this relationship?	What is your best course of action?	What is the deeper soul lesson you are learning in this relationship?

Remember, if the cards and your intuition suggest that the relationship isn't heading in the right direction, that doesn't mean you should ditch it immediately. Just be aware that there may be challenges ahead and stay open to the possibility that if you address those challenges proactively, you may be able to steer the relationship in the right direction and get it back on track.

LONG-TERM RELATIONSHIPS

It was the summer of 2006 and my husband-to-be and I were sitting on a patch of grass, looking out across the stunning botanical gardens in Melbourne and the lake below. We had a huge, blank piece of paper and our markers out.

"What's important to you in our relationship?" I asked him.

"Hmm, good question," he said.

Then he was silent for a while, before finally answering, "Communication. Intimacy. And openness."

"What does communication mean to you," I asked trying to get a little deeper.

"I guess it means talking about our feelings together openly, even if they're not good feelings. And keeping each other up-to-date on where we're at, even if we're feeling disconnected or unsure about things."

"What about you? What's important to you?" he asked.

"Freedom. To create a life of freedom together. And to give each other the freedom to be ourselves, even if that means having time on our own or doing some things independently of each other."

"Cool, I'm down with that. Let's write it down," he responded enthusiastically.

We wanted to talk about what was important to us, where our boundaries lay, and what we wanted from the future of our relationship. So we spent that afternoon having one of the best conversations we've ever had, sharing our hopes and dreams for the relationship, aligning our values, and forming new agreements as a couple for our relationship in the future—and out of that came our wedding vows.

DEEPENING LOVE—TOGETHER

· ⁕ ✳ ⁕ ·

Reading the Tarot together with your partner is a beautiful way to start a conversation about the kind of relationship you want to create and nurture together, regardless of whether he or she knows how to read the Tarot cards. This is a great exercise to do at major milestones in the relationship, like engagement, anniversaries, or even the New Year.

Before you start, make sure your partner is open to exploring the deeper levels of the relationship through a tool such as the Tarot. (If they are dead-set against it, skip this activity. You want your partner to be on board from the get-go.) You may need to create a safe space together, explaining how you'll work with the cards more as a conversation starter than a prediction tool. And explain how the imagery of the Tarot cards can help you both access a deeper part of yourself and will foster a better conversation.

Once you've done the groundwork, spread out the Tarot cards in front of you faceup. Together, consciously choose Tarot cards for the following questions:

1	2	3
What do I love and appreciate about you?	What do I love and appreciate about our relationship?	What is important to me in this relationship?

4	5	6
What am I missing in this relationship?	What do I want from the relationship in the future?	What soul lesson are we learning together?

You may find that you choose the same card, or different cards. Either is OK and will give you lots of insight into the relationship.

If you get stuck choosing a card, you can let your intuition guide you toward one.

As you go through each question, have a conversation about the cards you chose and why. Take turns in describing what you see in the card and what this means for the relationship. You might start to notice other things in the cards that deepen your conversation. Let the conversation flow where it needs to—even if it diverts from the Tarot cards you chose.

Compare the cards chosen to see where you share similar ideas about the relationship and where you might have differences. This works beautifully regardless of whether you know how to read Tarot because you are simply using the images to describe what you think and feel.

You might also like to create a vision board together for your dream relationship, using images, words, and feelings. Put it somewhere you'll see every day and watch as your dream relationship continues to blossom.

WHEN RELATIONSHIPS GET HARD

· ✳ ✱ ✳ ·

No matter how long you've been together or how much you love each other, there are bound to be times in your relationship when things get tough. It may be a heated argument, family issues, financial challenges, breaking trust agreements, or growing in different directions.

Often, it is a situation that can be overcome, so long as you and your partner are both committed to making it work. To help you do this, I have created the Resolving Conflict Tarot Spread that gives you deeper insight into the problems you're facing and how you can constructively move through this *together.*

1

What is at the heart of
this situation?

2

What is the impact
of this situation on
our relationship?

3

What is the underlying
lesson we are
learning here?

4

What is important to me
in this situation?

5

What is important to
my partner in this situation?

6

What does a successful
outcome look like?

7

How can we reach a
successful outcome?

8

What needs to change
within me to support a
successful outcome?

9

What needs to change
within my partner to
support a successful
outcome?

10

How will I know when
we are on track?

11

What might we
experience over the
coming weeks/months?

ENDING RELATIONSHIPS

"I want to be single again."

Ugh, those words stabbed deep into my heart like the Three of Swords, inflicting pain, hurt, and rejection.

I had just returned from a three-week trip around Australia looking after a group of foreign exchange students, only to be met by my boyfriend of two-and-a-half years telling me he wanted to be single. When he left, I cried so hard that I felt like it would never stop. Every thought, every memory ripped deeper and deeper into my soul. I thought I would never recover and my heart would remain broken forever. But, little by little, I loosened my grip, pried off my fingers, and started to regain a sense of who I was.

It took a good six months to feel ready to open up to new love after that breakup. Man, it was hard. But over time, I rediscovered myself. I took back my inner power. And I started to date again.

Many of us have experienced painful endings to our relationships. While this is a normal part of being human, it doesn't make them any less painful, and left unchecked, these past experiences can become triggers to shut down emotionally in future relationships.

Opening your heart to receive and give love can be scary. Moments of abandonment and disappointment can stick with us long after they occur and can cause real and damaging intimacy blocks. The problem is that if we want fulfilling, authentic relationships, we need to be vulnerable.

THE BREAKUP

Oh, sweet pea! If you're reading this part of the book, then you're no doubt going through a rough time right now. Here's a big virtual hug from me. I'm so sorry you're hurting.

When you are right in the middle of a breakup, it feels as if the sun will never shine again, and even the most basic tasks become seemingly impossible.

But I promise it won't feel like that forever. Time will heal a broken heart, and you are stronger than you know.

To help you deal with a breakup, here are two strategies using Tarot as a guide.

WHY DID WE BREAK UP?

After a breakup, you can sometimes be left with a lot of questions. Whether or not you were the one to end the relationship, this spread can help with the healing process. Ask the Tarot:

1	2	3
What did I bring to this relationship?	**What did my partner bring to this relationship?**	**Why did we break up?**

4	5	6
What could I have done differently?	**What can I learn from this experience?**	**How can I start to heal from this breakup?**

Keep in mind—especially when you are going through the early stages of a breakup—that you are likely to be feeling all sorts of emotions, including denial, anger, and sadness. This is one instance where you may benefit from doing the reading a few times to help you understand what happened and to allow the message to sink in fully. Give yourself time and space to process the reading with an open heart and open mind, and you'll start to receive the critical intuitive messages in the cards that will help you heal.

WILL I GET BACK WITH MY EX?

Even the strongest, most resilient people will have those momentary hopes of reuniting with their ex, especially while they are still recovering from the relationship. Let's be real, though: most times it's a bad idea. But hey, some-times you just have to be told that it's a bad idea before you can fully let go of the relationship and begin the path to healing.

So here's the "Will I Get Back with My Ex?" Spread to help you out:

1

What was our
relationship like before
we broke up?

2

Why did the
relationship come
to an end?

3

Where does
our relationship
stand now?

4

Why do I want
to get back
with my ex?

5

What do I want
from the future
relationship?

6

What does my
ex want from
the future
relationship?

7

What would
need to change
for the relation-
ship to work?

8

What might I
experience if we do get
back together?

9

What might I
experience if I choose
to move on?

10

What is the healthiest
version of our
relationship?

Remember, at the end of this reading, you have a choice: whether you pursue this relationship or whether you let it go. Once you have made your choice, commit to it even when things get tough and you second-guess yourself.

MOVING ON

You've made it through the toughest part of the breakup, and you're committed to putting this relationship behind you. So how do you heal yourself and move forward?

The following Healing Heart Spread will help you to clear out any unfinished business with your past relationship and focus on new opportunities.

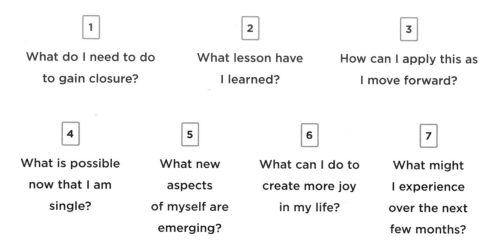

1	2	3
What do I need to do to gain closure?	What lesson have I learned?	How can I apply this as I move forward?

4	5	6	7
What is possible now that I am single?	What new aspects of myself are emerging?	What can I do to create more joy in my life?	What might I experience over the next few months?

You may also want to choose a Tarot card that represents how you want to feel as a newly single person. Perhaps you want to be like the Queen of Wands—radiant, confident, and sociable. Or perhaps you want to be resilient and strong like the Strength card. Or maybe this is your opportunity to take a spiritual journey to rediscover yourself, like the Hermit. Pick out a card and place it somewhere you can see every day as a reminder of what you are creating.

There are few areas in our lives where we need our intuition's guidance more than matters of the heart. The thoughts, emotions, fears, thrills—and yes, hormones—that flood our brains and bodies over the course of our love lives can be all-consuming—forget about thinking clearly!

Sitting down with your Tarot deck for even a few minutes offers a chance to ground and reconnect with yourself so you can move forward with intention. In the next chapter, we'll discuss creating a sacred space to nurture your most essential relationship—the one you have with your Higher Self.

CHAPTER 8

SACRED RITUALS WITH TAROT

OVER THE COURSE OF THIS BOOK, WE'VE DELVED INTO SOME OF THE biggest and most important areas of our lives: relationships, work, goals and big decisions. On any given day, I'm willing to bet that you've got something going on in one or even all of those spheres. Add in the busy-ness of living in the modern world—commutes, schedules, errands, laundry, stress . . . the list goes on and on—and it can get a little overwhelming. Even taking five minutes to do a Daily Tarot Card exercise sounds impossible!

Believe me when I tell you that creating *space* for yourself to sit quietly, away from all the noise, hustle, bustle, and expectations swirling around you, is one of the very best things you can do for yourself.

In this chapter, we'll talk about the importance of rituals, how they can be used for reflection, gratitude, and even transformation, and how creating a sacred ritual of your own is one of the most powerful things you can do. Here is where you take your spirituality and your intuition to the next level. We can pretend we're spiritual, but it's not until we put these sacred moments into place that we walk our talk.

Now, am I perfect at sacred ritual? No. I have many mornings where I spend my first hour scrolling through email and our team communications tool Slack. But when I start to feel out of sorts, coming back to sacred ritual helps ground me and bring me back into alignment.

WHAT IS RITUAL? AND WHY DO IT?

Ritual is traditionally defined as "a sequence of activities involving gestures, words, and objects, performed in a sequestered place, and performed according to a set sequence." That's how *Merriam-Webster's* puts it, but I tend to see ritual in a more informal light. It's a sacred, intuitive practice, sure, but it can also be as small as a moment to yourself where you can just *be*.

In fact, I bet you already have some informal rituals in your life.

How about making your cup of coffee in the morning? Or pouring yourself a glass of wine and watching your favorite show after the kids have been put to bed? Applying your makeup in the morning, or going for a run next to the water during your lunch break?

All of these are little quiet moments that are just for you, and I'm willing to bet they feel pretty integral to your happiness and well-being. I know they are for me!

Sacred rituals take it a bit deeper. They are a beautiful way to connect with your intuition, your pure potential, and your Higher Self. Through deep symbolism and soulful intention, they connect you to the Universal energy in a powerful and potent way.

This is the stuff that makes us more intuitive, that helps us live in alignment with who we are. Ritual helps you connect with your sacredness, your soul.

If we take a moment out of our busy lives to reconnect with spirit, we find our place of peace and calm easily. And it's from this place that we can connect with our intuition and let it be our guide in a meaningful way.

Many people think that a ritual is a set process you must follow; yet ritual is often at its most powerful when it is personalized and created with intention. Following what someone else tells you to do is not going to get the big results you want. You have to set the intention of what you want to create, and you have to think about how you can best set your intention in motion through ritual.

So I want you to approach the following rituals with Tarot as a starting point. You have my blessing to change and modify these rituals to make them personal and meaningful to you—because that's where you will find the most transformation.

"ANYTIME" RITUALS

Creating a daily connection with your Tarot cards allows you to generate a beautiful, sacred space to also connect with your intuition and your inner wisdom.

Whether you're doing this with Tarot cards, crystals, journaling, meditation, or something entirely different doesn't matter. The important thing is that you're making the time to go within and listen. That's where the answers are and that's how you can begin to create a fulfilling, purposeful life.

Everyday rituals don't always have to be lengthy, drawn-out processes. In fact, sometimes all you need is a couple of minutes out of your day to draw a Tarot card and reconnect with your inner wisdom to find peace again. Here are two quick rituals you can do anytime, anywhere.

THE "CALM ME DOWN" RITUAL

Anytime you feel a little frazzled, unfocused, emotional, or confused, take a moment to ground yourself with a Tarot card.

First, take in a couple of deep breaths and become aware of the seat beneath you. Feel the weight of your body on the chair and your feet on the ground connecting you to the earth.

Then, draw a card from your Tarot deck and ask, "What am I experiencing right now?"

The intention of this card is not to determine why you're feeling this way or how you can fix the situation. It is simply to refocus you on the present moment and allow you to become more mindful of your current circumstance.

THE "HIGHER SELF HOTLINE" RITUAL

· * ✳ * ·

This Higher Self Hotline is perfect when you're faced with a difficult decision, dealing with a challenging person, or you just want to dial in your intuition on an important matter but don't want to do a full Tarot reading.

Take in a deep breath to clear your mind, and then draw one Tarot card from the deck, asking for guidance for your particular situation. Reflect on the card's message and combine it with your intuitive feel for the situation for extra guidance. Then, choose one action you will take to bring about a resolution to your problem.

DAILY SUN RITUALS

When my husband and I were traveling in the North End of Australia (pre-kids), we stopped off in Darwin, which, among other things, is renowned for its stunning sunsets. One evening, we headed to the beach, keen to catch the sun setting for the day. Thinking we'd be the only ones down at the beach, we were surprised to see hundreds of people on the sand, with picnics, blankets, even sing-alongs, all waiting for the sun to set. As the sun got closer and closer to the horizon, the sky lit up with the most beautiful pinks and purples. It was as if this were Mother Earth's canvas and She was creating the most stunning, moving artwork for us all to admire. Finally, the sun crept lower and lower until the shining ball of light disappeared into the ocean. And then, everyone started clapping in sincere appreciation for this beautiful event.

My heart was radiating with gratitude, and it brings tears to my eyes even now. Here was this natural occurrence that was so amazing and we had all forgotten about it—until that moment. We get so wrapped up in getting home from work or making dinner or getting the kids ready for bed that we forget to honor and appreciate this beautiful scene from nature. And yet, for whatever reason, here were 200+ people sitting on the beach, honoring this daily spectacle. It made my heart sing.

So now it's your turn. Take these two miracle moments every day—sunrise and sunset—and turn them into two powerful rituals to help you expand into your fullest potential and give thanks for what you have created.

THE SUNRISE EXPANSION RITUAL

· * ✳ * ·

Do this ritual as close to sunrise as possible, and ideally in the light of the rising sun. If your sunrise isn't at the most convenient time, then do it upon waking up.

Close your eyes and take a deep breath in, drinking in the energy of the sun. Then as you breathe out, feel that warm flow of energy radiating through your body. Take two more deep breaths like this, filling up with the sun's radiant energy.

Take this time to meditate on one of the following questions:

✳   **What do I most look forward to today?**

✳   **How can I expand into my fullest potential today?**

✳   **What is emerging for me today?**

See what comes to you intuitively. You might see a symbol, hear a word or phrase, get a feeling, or know something. Be curious as to what your intuition wants to show you.

Then, gently open your eyes, and when you're ready, pull a Tarot card asking the same question. What new insights does the card give you? And what actions can you take to make the most of the day ahead?

Write down your thoughts and insight into your journal.

THE SUNSET GRATITUDE RITUAL

· ✳ ·

Do this ritual as close to sunset as possible, and ideally where you can view the sky. If the timing is not convenient, then do it as you go to bed.

Close your eyes and take a deep breath. As you breathe out, feel a gentle flow of relaxation go through your body. Take two more deep breaths, relaxing more and more each time.

Now, ask yourself, "What am I truly grateful for today?"

See what comes to you intuitively. Be curious as to what your intuition wants to show you.

Then, gently open your eyes, and when you're ready, pull a Tarot card asking the same question. What new insights does the card give you?

Finally, write down your thoughts and insights into your journal.

Continue to do both the Sunrise and Sunset Rituals each day, especially when it feels like life is rushing by. It will bring you a greater sense of calm and peace in the long term.

MONTHLY MOON RITUALS

If the moon has the power to create the ebb and flow of the ocean's tides, it no doubt also has the power to influence human beings, especially as we are 60 percent water. Paying attention to the moon cycles by setting intentions at the new moon and releasing and letting go at the full moon is a powerful way to align with the Universe—and ourselves. Using the lunar cycles allows you to recharge and recalibrate your energy in alignment with the Universal energies that are flowing around you.

The new moon and the week leading up to the new moon are a magical time for setting intentions and manifesting new beginnings. And the full moon is the perfect time for honoring your achievements and releasing what no longer serves you.

To support you in the process, I have created two powerful rituals for you to perform—one on the new moon and one on the full moon.

Each ritual also includes a transformative visualization, allowing you to connect with your Higher Self and bring the energy of the moon into your daily life.

The key to performing these rituals is to be fully present with an open heart, an open mind, and a willingness to be open to all possibilities.

NEW MOON RITUAL

· ✳ ✦ ✳ ·

The best time to do the New Moon Ritual is on the new moon or in the days leading up to the new moon. Check the lunar phases for your local area at www.timeanddate.com/moon/phases.

Download the New Moon Visualization to your audio player from www.everydaytarot.com/free so it's ready to go (or read the text on page 198).

Find a space where you will not be disturbed for at least thirty minutes. Outside is ideal, but if that's not possible, then inside will work just fine.

Gather your tools—your Tarot cards, a pen and notebook, candles, smudge stick, crystals, your audio player for the visualization, and anything else you feel called to have with you for the ritual.

CREATE A SACRED SPACE

Create a small altar with your favorite things or lay out a crystal grid, whatever you feel called to do to create a beautiful sacred space.

Light your candles and dim the lights.

Light your smudge stick and gently wave the smoke over the front and back of your body, as you clear and cleanse your aura.

DO THE NEW MOON
MANIFESTATION TAROT SPREAD

Take out your Tarot cards and do this simple, yet powerful spread:

| 1 | 2 | 3 |

What have I released
since the full moon?

Where am I now?

What is emerging
within me?

| 4 | 5 | 6 |

What do I wish
to grow?

How can I bring my
goals and intentions
to fruition?

What additional
resources are available
to me as I manifest
my goals?

Record the reading in your notebook and write down your key insights.

SET YOUR INTENTIONS

Holding the energy of your New Moon Tarot Reading, write down your intentions for the next lunar cycle. What do you want to create this cycle? What
new opportunities do you want to tap into?

DO THE NEW MOON VISUALIZATION

Find a comfortable position. While laying down may feel most comfortable,
if you are prone to falling asleep during a visualization, then I recommend
sitting upright.

Play the visualization you downloaded from www.everydaytarot.com/
free through your audio player. It will take ten minutes.

After the visualization, write down your experience and any intuitive
insights that you received.

CLOSE OUT THE RITUAL

At this stage, check in with yourself and your intuition to see if there is any other activity you need to do before closing out the ritual. For example, you may feel called to say a personal affirmation out loud three times, spend some time chanting, or even start dancing to your favorite song. Go with your instincts on this one.

When the ritual feels complete, close the circle by giving thanks to your guides and your intuition. Say out loud, "And so it is done!"

Blow out the candles and gently turn the lights back on, returning to your everyday life once again.

FULL MOON RITUAL

· * ✳ * ·

The best time to do the Full Moon Ritual is on the full moon or in the days leading up to the full moon. Check the lunar phases for your local area at www.timeanddate.com/moon/phases.

Download the Full Moon Visualization to your audio player from www.everydaytarot.com/free so it's ready to go (or read the text on page 200).

Find a space where you will not be disturbed for at least thirty minutes. Outside is ideal, but if that's not possible, then inside is fine.

Gather your tools—your Tarot cards, a pen and notebook as well as a separate sheet of paper, candles, smudge stick, crystals, your audio player for the visualization, matches, a fireproof bowl, and anything else you feel called to have with you for the ritual.

CREATE A SACRED SPACE

Create a small altar with your favorite things or lay out a crystal grid, whatever you feel called to do to create a beautiful sacred space.

Place your fireproof bowl on the altar with the matches nearby.

Light your candles and dim the lights.

Light your smudge stick and gently wave the smoke over the front and back of your body, as you clear and cleanse your aura.

DO THE FULL MOON TAROT SPREAD

Take out your Tarot cards and do this simple, yet powerful spread:

1	2	3
What have I created and manifested since the new moon?	Where am I now?	What is coming into my conscious awareness?

4	5	6
What is no longer serving me?	How can I release and let go of these energies?	What additional resources are available to me as I release and let go?

Record the reading in your notebook and write down your key insights.

HONOR YOUR ACHIEVEMENTS

Reflect on the intentions you set during the previous new moon. What did you create and manifest? And what new opportunities emerged?

Write these down in your journal, honoring each achievement as you go. Give thanks for what you have created and learned along the way.

DO THE FULL MOON VISUALIZATION

Find a comfortable position. While laying down may feel most comfortable, if you are prone to falling asleep during a visualization, then I recommend sitting upright.

Play the visualization downloaded from www.everydaytarot.com/free through your audio player. It will take ten minutes.

After the visualization, write down your experience and any intuitive insights that you received.

RELEASE AND LET GO (OPTIONAL)

In the Full Moon Visualization, you are invited to release and let go of that which does not serve you. If you feel complete after the visualization, then skip this step. But if you think you have more to let go of, or it would be helpful to do the Release and Let Go Ritual in the physical realm, then go ahead with this step.

Write down what is no longer serving you and what energies you want to release on the separate sheet of paper. Give yourself a reasonable amount of time to fully express yourself until it feels that there is nothing else left.

Light this piece of paper with a match over the fireproof bowl. As it burns, say out loud:

> *"I release and let go of any excess energy that no longer*
> *serves me. Through Divine Will and unconditional love,*
> *so be it."*

Once the paper has finished burning, affirm out loud, "I release you. I am done."

Take a moment to experience this feeling of release fully.

CLOSE OUT THE RITUAL

At this stage, check in with yourself and your intuition to see if there is any other activity you need to do before closing out the ritual. For example, you may feel called to shake off any residual energy, to write a letter of forgiveness, or to meditate with your favorite crystal. Go with your instincts on this one.

When the ritual feels complete, close the circle by giving thanks to your guides and your intuition. Say out loud, "And so it is done!"

Blow out the candles and gently turn the lights back on, returning to your everyday life once again.

THE "I'M NOT GOING TO FREAK OUT BECAUSE IT'S MERCURY RETROGRADE" RITUAL

Mercury Retrograde gets a bad rap, that's for sure. Three to four times a year the planet Mercury appears to move backward for three to four weeks, and during this time, things are known to go a little haywire. Mercury rules communication, travel, technology, and the legal system so when Mercury is in retrograde, these areas of life are at their absolute weakest point. Delays, miscommunications, technical breakdowns, rework, and just all-around craziness are all expected during a Mercury Retrograde.

But just between you and me, I think many people—myself included—use Mercury Retrograde as an excuse for the usual challenges we face in our busy world. Did the computer break down? Oh, it must be Mercury Retrograde! Did you send a raunchy email intended for your boyfriend to your mum? Oops, damn you, Mercury Retrograde! Train late again?! It's not me; it's Mercury Retrograde.

I'm as guilty of the planetary blame game as anyone, but something I've come to realize is that chalking every issue up to Mercury Retrograde is, well, lazy. And it ignores another important truth: Mercury Retrograde doesn't have to be *all bad*. In fact, it can be used for good!

Mercury Retrograde is the perfect time for revisiting, reworking, revising, reconsidering, reevaluating. Basically "re-" anything.

So instead of freaking out next time Mercury goes into retrograde, or conveniently blaming things on the planets, be prepared with this Mercury Retrograde Ritual.

Do this ritual within three days of the beginning of Mercury Retrograde. (A quick Google search will find you the dates for the next one.)

You'll need:

✳   Tarot cards

✳   Crystals—smoky quartz and/or black tourmaline to release any negative energy or anxiety, clear quartz for mental clarity and focus, and amazonite for clear communication

✳   A black candle symbolizing the release of negative energy

✳   A carving tool (e.g., a skewer, bobby pin, or sturdy pen)

✳   Matches

✳   Pen and paper

✳   A quiet space where you won't be interrupted

Lay out everything you need before you start, so it is within arm's reach.

Close your eyes and take a few deep breaths to center and ground yourself. When you're ready, open your eyes.

Take the black candle and your carving tool and carefully carve the mercury symbol into the candle.

Light the candle, and as you do, know that this candle represents your intention to release any negativity associated with Mercury Retrograde and your willingness to embrace the opportunities to reassess, rework, revisit, and reconnect with whatever needs your attention during this period.

Next, place your crystals around the candle, and as you do, set the intention to release negative energy with smoky quartz and black tourmaline, to create mental clarity and focus with clear quartz, and to communicate clearly and compassionately with amazonite. (If you love your crystals, you might add in a few more that have personal significance for you.)

Now, pull out your Tarot cards and draw a card for each of the following:

| 1 | 2 | 3 | 4 |

What will this
Mercury
Retrograde
bring into my
awareness?

How will this
Mercury
Retrograde
affect me?

What do I need
to revisit during
this Mercury
Retrograde?

What do I need
to rework during
this Mercury
Retrograde?

| 5 | 6 |

What unknown factors do I
need to be aware of?

What precautions can I take for a
smooth Mercury Retrograde?

Write down each card you drew and the insights you received. Create a list of two to three actions you will take to make the most of this Mercury Retrograde period.

Finally, ask the Tarot, "What is my soul lesson during this Mercury Retrograde?" Keep this particular card in a visible place throughout the Mercury Retrograde period as a reminder of how this time is here to serve you. You may also see the card's deeper message unfold and emerge as you move through Mercury Retrograde, so keep coming back to how it relates to you.

Close out the ritual by thanking your Higher Self and by saying out loud the following affirmation:

"I give thanks for Mercury Retrograde and the opportunity to reassess, rework, revisit, and reconnect with that which needs my attention. I speak my truth with loving assertiveness. I listen to what others are really trying to communicate to me. I am centered and calm. And I am vigilant and attentive when it comes to the details. As in all my life, my intuition guides me to make the best decisions for my Highest Good. Through Divine Will and unconditional love, so be it."

Blow out the candle and get ready for an awesome Mercury Retrograde. (Yes, it *is* possible!)

NEW YEAR RITUAL

This New Year Ritual is a beautiful, empowering way to begin your year! You'll be connecting with your Higher Self and envisioning what you truly want to manifest in the year to come. This is about positive change and transformation at a deep, symbolic level that will help you create an abundant, super-charged year ahead!

To give your New Year Ritual that extra energetic boost, I recommend doing the ritual between the New Moon and the Full Moon, on either side of the New Year.

You can, of course, use this New Year Ritual at any time of the year, especially around birthdays, anniversaries, and other times of transition or change.

BEFORE YOU START

Before you begin your New Year Ritual, you'll need the following:

- ✳ **Your favorite Tarot deck**

- ✳ **Your favorite markers**

- ✳ **At least one candle and some matches**

- ✳ **A sage smudge stick**

- ✳ **Items for your altar. These are symbols of what you want to create in the new year such as an image of your ideal relationship, a flower for beauty, a seedpod for starting something new—you choose!**

- ✳ **At least one hour of uninterrupted time. Lock the door, turn off your phone, do whatever you need to protect your sacred space.**

- ✳ **Your favorite crystals. I recommend citrine for abundance and clear quartz for clarity.** *(Optional)*

THE NEW YEAR RITUAL
· * ✳ * ·

STEP 1:
Create the Sacred Space

Get everything you need for the ritual, then create your sacred space.

Set up your altar. This doesn't have to be super-fancy. Just place the items you collected that represent what you want to create in the new year. Add in crystals, Tarot cards, jewelry, flowers, rocks—whatever helps you to set a sacred intention for your ritual.

Place the candles in and around your altar. And when you are ready, switch off the lights and light the candles.

Take a moment to ground yourself. Close your eyes and take in a few deep breaths. Connect with the earth's energy and the Universal energy, feeling yourself filled with a beautiful white light.

STEP 2:
Reflect on the Past Year

Reflect on the year that has just ended. What did you experience? What were the highs? What were the lows? And what did you learn along the way? Use the Tarot cards to help you go deeper with each question, and then write down your insights in your notebook or journal.

Now, reflect on what you want to release and let go of from the past year. Again, use your Tarot cards if you get stuck, and write down your thoughts.

Take the sage smudge stick and light it. Then, wave the smoke around your body, front and back, as you cleanse your aura and release any old energy that may be clinging to you. For each item on your list, say aloud, "I release myself of . . . (insert what you want to release)."

When you feel complete, say aloud three times, "I give thanks for the past year. I release what no longer serves me. And I welcome new opportunities with open arms."

STEP 3:
Visualize What You Want to Create in the New Year

Now, close your eyes and start to imagine what you want to create in the coming year.

Think about what you want to nurture in your relationships. Imagine it as if it were a movie in your mind, experiencing everything you want to experience in your relationships in the next twelve months. See yourself in the movie, being an active participant. See what you see. Hear what you hear. Feel what you feel. Taste what you taste. And smell what you smell. Create a full sensory experience.

When you're ready, wipe the movie screen clean, and bring up a new movie, this time about your career, work, and finances. What do you want to create in your material world? Create a full sensory experience.

When you're complete, bring up the next movie for your health and well-being. And after that, run one for your personal development. What do you want to create?

When you feel complete, open your eyes, and write down your experiences.

Next, take out your Tarot cards and draw one card each for relationships, career and finances, health and well-being, and personal development. Take note of the cards you drew and your insights in your notebook.

STEP 4:
Choose a Theme for the Year

It can be very powerful to choose a keyword or phrase as your theme for the year and then follow that theme throughout the year. For example, in 2016, my word was "abundance," and in that year, I doubled my business, signed a book deal, and manifested my dream home and paid off the mortgage within six months.

You might already have an idea of what your theme will be for the year ahead. If not, draw a Tarot card (or three) and brainstorm some ideas. Then, pick one. And write it down.

Close your eyes and take a moment to feel into that word. What does it look and feel like when you have that word present in your life?

STEP 5:
Manifest Your Goals for the New Year

Choose ten things you want to manifest in the next twelve months. For example, I want to be fit and healthy, or I want to take a three-month vacation.

Then, change these to "I am" statements—yes, even if they sound a little funny. For example, "I *am* fit and healthy" or "I *am* a three-month vacation."

Take a moment to feel the energy and the vibration of these "I am" statements—super-powerful, right?

Draw a Tarot card for each of the statements, asking for guidance on how you can manifest these goals.

STEP 6:
Create Your Monthly Forecast

Create a twelve-month forecast for the year ahead by drawing a Tarot card for every month. Each card represents the theme for that month. Don't be put off if you see a "negative" card one month—instead, see it as something you can be aware of and prepare for so that you can make the most of the time ahead.

Remember to write down each Tarot card you draw and the insights and lessons you see in the card. You might also start to notice a flow throughout the year, as one card leads into the next. Look out for these prominent themes and patterns.

STEP 7:
Close the Space

Close your eyes and visualize a ball of bright, white light radiating from your solar plexus just above your belly button. Imagine the ball of light getting bigger and bigger, filling your body, flowing through your aura, and radiating out into the world. This is your power, your determination, your ability to manifest your goals, just as you see it. And so it is done. When you are ready, gently open your eyes.

Before you close the space, check in with your Higher Self and ask if there is anything else that needs to get done before this ritual is complete. Sometimes your intuition may guide you to another sacred activity before you know for sure that you are finished.

When you're ready, say a prayer of thanks to your Higher Self for guiding you through this process. Then, say out loud, "And so it is so."

Blow out the candles, turn on the lights, and pack up the space. You may wish to leave part of your altar there or move it somewhere more convenient, so you have a visual reminder of this beautiful ritual that you have given to yourself.

CREATE YOUR OWN TAROT RITUAL

In 2015, I spent three months traveling with my family in Spain. Inspired by the beauty and sheer power of the Spanish Pyrenees, I decided to journey out one afternoon with my Tarot cards, a notepad, and pen, with the intention of connecting with nature and ultimately my Divine Guidance System.

I allowed myself to be led to a place in nature. I roughly knew where I wanted to go, but once I arrived in the general area, I allowed myself to be guided to the exact spot that held the most energy for me. This is just part of the tuning in process and allowing yourself to hear what your intuition has to say.

Before starting the ritual, I found some stones and placed them in a circle as my sacred space. I also found some pinecones and wildflowers to decorate the circle, as a way to honor the natural environment. And finally, I placed everything I would need within that circle: Tarot cards, water, pen and paper, and iPhone (for the camera only!).

I sat in the circle, closed my eyes, and cleared my mind. I brought my attention inward, grounding myself through the earth and connecting with the Universe through a bright, white light from above.

I became aware of my surroundings, feeling the wind as a symbol of the element of Air, the sun as a symbol of Fire, the ground as a symbol of Earth, and drinking the water I had collected from a nearby stream as a symbol of Water.

When I felt ready, I opened my eyes and picked up my Tarot cards and shuffled.

I wasn't exactly sure what to ask, but again, I let myself be guided to what felt right. In this case, I was drawn to ask simply for an "Opening" card. I drew the Eight of Pentacles.

"Doing the work," I heard.

I had to laugh. Yes, indeed, I was doing the work.

I wanted to go deeper, so I asked the Tarot how I could move beyond thinking about work and cherish this adventure with my family. This time I drew Justice reversed.

The message I received was that I needed to find inner balance. It was time to meditate again.

I cleared my mind, grounded myself, and connected to the Universe once again. This time, I became aware of the wind moving through the trees, and instantly thought, "Spirit moves through us." Beautiful. Now I was going deeper.

I felt compelled to ask the Tarot, "What message does my soul have for me?" I drew the Nine of Pentacles reversed.

This time, I invited my soul to speak through free writing. That is, I simply wrote down what came to mind, without stopping.

The insights were very powerful and enlightening to me on a personal level. Here's a taste:

My Soul Speaks . . .

Nine of Pentacles reversed

Self-worth, richness, abundance

Cultivated nature-wanting nature to be perfect & pristine

but knowing it can be messy, "organic"

Not everything has to be perfect, polished, "beautiful"

Allow things to evolve naturally, messily, by turning inwards

Forget about outward appearance

Beauty on the inside

Spiritual & financial richness, wealth

Let go & let things unfold

Move at a snail's pace-slow down.

Wealth doesn't have to come all at once

The next question I felt guided to ask was, "What is emerging in my life?" I drew the Temperance card.

Again, I allowed myself to write in the flow with more powerful insights about my personal journey:

What is emerging in my life?

Temperence

Patience—I'm on the right path. It's a process of balancing
& rebalancing, checking in, flattening out

Being in flow—from one side to the other. Never quite in
perfect balance or harmony—but that is not the idea

Gently moving through light & shade, ebb, flow

Nothing is in perfect balance—and that's OK!!

Ebb & flow leads to the chosen path. A bit of this, a bit of that

Stay connected to the universe & you will always be guided
towards your path, navigating the bumps along the road—
and it is bumpy. BUT THAT'S OK

It was after this that I noticed a little black beetle nearby, making his way slowly, but surely, over and under each grass blade. It drew me back to the slow journey of the snail in the Nine of Pentacles and the undulating, never-in-perfect-balance-but-still-okay path of the Temperance card.

This was indeed where Tarot and nature blended, to connect me even more deeply to my Divine Guidance System and my intuition. Such is the beauty of the Tarot in Nature Ritual.

It reminded me that nothing is ever in perfect balance—and that's okay. I don't have to be perfectly "spiritual" or perfectly "entrepreneurial" or perfectly "motherly." I can move through each aspect of myself gently, and when it feels like too much, I move on into the next aspect to balance things out. It's this ongoing, undulating journey that will get me to where I want to go. It's very reassuring indeed.

With this insight, I was ready to close the ritual out. I drew one final "Closing" card—the Page of Swords. Communication. Clarity. Action.

And I couldn't help but be impressed again with the connection between the Page and my immediate surroundings:

I wrapped up with a sense of gratitude to nature, to Tarot, to my intuition, and ultimately, to the Universe, for giving me such a beautiful, joyful experience. And with that, the ritual was complete.

The beauty of creating your own ritual is that you don't have to be a master of Tarot, magic, or ritual to get the most out of the experience. The whole intention of the ritual is to get you in tune with your intuition to manifest a specific intention.

PAGE OF SWORDS

What's more, you can use this ritual to get to know the Tarot cards on a profound and personal level. When you're in a heightened state of awareness, you let your intuition do the talking, and the Tarot cards begin to "speak" to you in ways you have never heard before.

YOUR MOST POWERFUL RITUAL

· ✳ ·

Rituals become even more powerful when *you* create them.

When you set an intention and create a ritual to manifest that intention, that's where the magic happens and you see real results. The ritual has a part of you in it, a part of your soul. It is imbued with your personal power.

Creating a powerful ritual of your own is as easy as setting an intention and honoring that intention through symbolic actions. It can be as simple as lighting a candle and choosing an intention, or it might be something much more elaborate, conducted over several days, weeks, or even months. It's entirely up to you. Don't worry—I have your back and will guide you through the steps to creating your own Tarot rituals. And I give you my blessing to "color outside of the lines" and create rituals that may incorporate other things too.

This is where you get to be super-creative, intuitive, and in flow! Take flight, my friend!

TRADITIONAL RITUALS OR SOMETHING ELSE?

Different religions and esoteric traditions will have their own specific ways of conducting a ritual. What I recommend throughout this chapter does not represent these traditional rituals. Instead, I've chosen to focus on intuitively led, personalized rituals, as I believe the power of intention is what matters.

FIVE STEPS TO CREATING
YOUR OWN TAROT RITUALS
· * ✳ * ·

STEP 1:
Set an Intention

Most rituals serve the purpose of manifesting a goal or intention.

Think about what it is you want to create in your life right now. It might be more self-love, compassion, or joy. It might be that you want to manifest your dream home, start a successful business, or discover your soul purpose.

It doesn't have to be just about manifesting or creating. Sometimes your intention might be to release or remove something in your life.

STEP 2:
Create Your Altar

Your altar is your sacred space where you place items that are symbolic of what you want to create in your ritual. How you create your altar is up to you. You might lay out a special cloth on a table and place your favorite candles, crystals, and other sacred objects on top.

Choose items for your altar that also symbolize your intention for the ritual. For example, in a Self-Love Ritual, you may include rose quartz, known for its loving powers, essential oils such as ylang-ylang and rose, a photo of you where you felt joyful and refreshed, or even rose petals in the shape of a heart with your photo in the middle. You might also like to go through your Tarot deck and choose one card that represents the intention you wish to manifest. For

self-love, that might be the Nine of Pentacles, the Queen of Cups, or any other card that truly symbolizes your vision of loving and respecting yourself fully. Place the card on the altar.

Just before you start the ritual, you might like to smudge yourself with a sage stick, clearing your energy and preparing for a beautiful, connected ritual. Light the smudge stick, and wave the smoke over your body before extinguishing the stick in a fireproof bowl.

STEP 3:
Open the Circle

Now it is time to open the circle. The "circle" is your safe and sacred space in which you'll perform your ritual.

Close your eyes and take in a few deep breaths to center and ground yourself. Then imagine a ball of bright white light radiating from your heart center. The ball of light gets bigger and brighter every time you breathe in. It starts to fill every cell in your body, and then it expands out into your aura and the space around you, until you find yourself sitting in this sphere of bright, white light. Within this sphere of light you are protected, you are safe, and you are connected to the Universe and your Higher Self.

Gently open your eyes. Then, if you have a candle on your altar, light it, and as you do, say out loud:

"This sacred circle is now open. This sacred space is for divine healing, alignment, and manifestation for the Highest Good. It will remain open for the duration of this divine work. So be it."

Note: There are more traditional ways to open or "cast" a circle, such as calling in the four directions or reciting specific incantations. If you wish to use these methods, you have my blessing. However, I have chosen to keep things simple for this process, since I want you to be personally connected to your ritual and only do things you fully understand or resonate with.

STEP 4:
Perform the Ritual

This is the fun part! Let your intuition guide you to what you need to do to symbolize the manifestation of your intention.

To help get you started, here are a few ideas:

* ✳ Draw a Tarot card or do a Tarot reading to help you manifest your intention. For example, the Self-Love Tarot Reading would be perfect in a Self-Love Ritual.

* ✳ Set a timer for ten minutes and write continuously in your journal about your intention. You might write a love letter to yourself or what self-love means to you.

* ✳ Choose colored candles and speak out loud your intention as you light each candle. Pink is perfect for self-love!

* ✳ Close your eyes and visualize what it will be like when your intention comes to fruition. Create a full sensory experience in your mind by exploring what it will look like, sound like, smell like, feel like, and taste like when you have manifested your intention. For self-love, you might imagine yourself surrounded by pink, loving light as you envision what a typical day might be like when you fully and unconditionally love yourself.

* ✳ Put on your favorite music and dance in your sacred space as you hold your intention in your mind. For self-love, you might choose "Just The Way You Are" by Bruno Mars.

If you get a little stuck, check in with your Tarot cards. Ask them, "What do I need to include in this ritual?" You may get a few more ideas from what you pull.

Now, you can do just one of these things or even three or four. It's totally up to you. After you complete one step, check in with yourself and ask if you feel complete or whether it would be helpful to do another activity within your ritual. If you start to feel restless, "full," or simply ready to move on, then you know you're done!

STEP 5:
Close the Circle

To close the circle, close your eyes and imagine the sphere of white light around you is now fading into the ground. All that remains is a beautiful sense of peace and joy within you.

Open your eyes and say out loud:

> *"The sacred circle is now closed. All excess energy is released and sent to where it can do the most good. I give thanks to the Universe and my Higher Self for being open and present in this ritual. With gratitude and confidence, I acknowledge that this sacred work is now done. So be it."*

Blow out your candles, if you have any.

At this stage, it helps to ground yourself. Stand up, shake your arms and legs, jump up and down, or dance for a few minutes. You might also eat or drink something (I love some chocolate after sacred work). Then, walk away from the physical space where you have done your spiritual work, and carry on with your day or evening.

No matter how or when you choose to practice sacred ritual, it is my hope that you "do the work" of deepening your practice in this way. Whether it be for gratitude, reflection, healing, or transformation, I know that it will impact your life for the better—and that has been my goal for you and this book all along.

EVERYDAY TAROT

I was in a small, crowded room in the heart of Melbourne with thirty other soul-seekers, and each of us was entranced in a deep and moving meditation. With our eyes closed, we moved our bodies to the music, deeply engaged in our personal experiences and visions.

In my mind's eye, I first saw myself in a long line of women, dressed in black robes and connected by a chain. We were in a small room within the confines of a large enclosure in the middle of a desert over a thousand years ago. I realized we were part of a harem, stripped of our power and forced to do what we were told, but inside each of us was a spark—of inspiration, joy, and a power that no one could take away.

Then, the music changed and got louder.

"Some of those that work forces are the same that burn crosses."

I sensed myself transporting through time to four hundred years ago. Still female but now in a different body and a new setting, I realized I had a special gift of inner knowing and intuition. Except something was wrong; the patriarchy wanted to take my power. My gift was a threat.

Again I had that same sensation of being trapped and held back from expressing myself.

"Killing in the name of . . ."

We were about to be burned at the stake to stop our true power from coming through, because we were a threat to those in charge.

"Now you do what they told ya."

We had a choice: repent and banish ourselves from our intuition and inner guidance as we were ordered. Or we could rise.

"Fuck you, I won't do what you tell me."

Anger, rage, and an immense sense of power filled every cell of my body. My movement became stronger. Tears rolled down my cheeks. My arms were shaking.

"Fuck you, I won't do what you tell me."

Rise, Sister. Rise! Deep within my soul, I knew it was time to rise and let no one, *no one*, take away my power. And it was time to rise for my sisters and let no one take away their power.

Feelings of empowerment, drive, ambition, focus, and purpose were surging inside me—higher and higher—until my eyes burst open, and I knew. I knew why I was here.

From that moment on, I have been driven to help others connect with their intuition, to step into their power the same way I found mine. And I am fiercely opposed to anyone who may try to take it away.

There will be no more belittling the "woo-woo" or those things we can't fully grasp, no more telling us we're silly for listening to our gut. Now it's about trusting our inner guidance, knowing our power, and reclaiming our place in the community.

It drives through my work in Biddy Tarot. It is what inspired the writing in these pages.

Before my meditative experience, I was questioning my commitment to continuing my work I had felt bored and uninspired, but seeing this vision of what I am here to do, I knew I couldn't give up on what I was creating.

I know now that my work here, in this lifetime, is essential, and I will not stop until my job is done and every single person on the planet knows they can trust their inner wisdom and access their inner guidance whenever they need it. The drive, the power, the freedom, and strength I experienced that night swells from inside me. I am my own wellspring—and so are you. You no longer have to rely on external sources—authorities, hierarchies, patriarchies—to tell you what to do, give you what you want, or define your success. *All* of it comes from within you.

THINK IT'S ABOUT THE TAROT?
IT'S REALLY SOMETHING ELSE . . .

When you first picked this book up, no doubt you looked at the cover and thought, "Hey, this looks like an interesting book about the Tarot!" And I hope it is.

But I need to be honest with you: This book isn't about the Tarot.

It is a book about *you*—a book about trusting your inner wisdom, reclaiming your power, creating your future, and reconnecting with who you are.

Tarot is merely a way in, a way to help your conscious mind feel loved and nurtured while your subconscious mind and your intuition awaken through the pictures and meanings of the cards. You may think you're just doing a Tarot reading, but you're actually listening deeply to your inner voice and connecting with your Higher Self. You are learning more about *you*. Who are you? Why are you here? What lights you up?

And whether you're learning about yourself through Tarot cards, crystals, journaling, meditation—or something entirely different—it doesn't matter. The important thing is that you're making the time to listen. That's how you'll find the answers you seek and create a fulfilling, purposeful life.

Everyday Tarot is about integrating your intuition into your life and creating space for your inner wisdom to shine out. How will you do that?

Everyday Tarot is about the never-finished work of self-discovery, healing, and aligning with your Higher Self. What will you learn?

Everyday Tarot is about your soul purpose and stepping into your power to consciously create the life you want. What will you create?

I hope that this book lit a spark for you—a spark of inspiration, joy, and power that can never be taken away. I can't wait to see what you will do with it.

Much love,

LET'S STAY IN TOUCH

I love connecting with intuitively inspired, purpose-driven people who read Tarot. So let's stay in touch! You'll find me at www.biddytarot.com.

And if you want to take your connection with Tarot further, then access the free Everyday Tarot Reader Resources at www.everydaytarot.com/free and check out my courses and programs at www.biddytarot.com/shop.

BE PART OF THE EVERYDAY TAROT MOVEMENT

Join the growing tribe of people who are making Tarot and intuition part of their everyday life. Post your spreads, intuitive insights, and ideas to Instagram and Facebook with #everydaytarot.

GRATITUDE

You know the saying, "It takes a village to raise a child"? Well, it most certainly takes a village—even a global community—to birth a book. And for that I give thanks.

It has been beautiful to see so many people coming together in their own unique ways to ensure that this book has been birthed in its purest, most authentic format. It may have my name on the front, but this book is truly a culmination of many people's contributions, great and small.

I offer gratitude to . . .

My book agent, Laura Lee Mattingly, for believing in me and encouraging me to take this leap of faith into writing and publishing a book. And to literary agent Kathleen Rushall who first planted the seed that I ought to write a book.

My developmental editor, Ann Maynard, who turned my raw words into a beautiful, heartfelt story. She was my cheerleader, rescuer, and zen master throughout the writing process. And to Azul Terronez, my book coach, for holding me accountable to my schedule and reassuring me I would make my deadline without breaking a sweat.

The team at Running Press—Shannon Connors Fabricant, Ashley Benning, Susan Van Horn, and Amy Cianfrone—who connected with my vision for *Everyday Tarot* and elevated it to the next level with careful editing and beautiful design. And to Eleanor Grosch, our illustrator, for becoming immersed in the visual expression of the book and the Tarot cards and creating beautiful designs.

My team at Biddy Tarot, who have offered their unwavering support every step of the way, not only while I was writing this book, but also in building Biddy Tarot. They took care of business and fiercely protected my time so I could write solidly for two months, and they have helped make Biddy Tarot what it is today.

My business buddies, Emily Thompson and Kathleen Shannon, for walking ahead of me and lighting up the path of publishing a book, and Maia Toll, Nicole Cody, Kate McKibbin, and Jenny Shih for providing moral support on our regular masterminding calls. And to my business coaches and mentors, Jadah Sellner, James Schramko, Stephanie Pollack, and Rachna Jain, who helped me see my unlimited potential and encouraged me to lean into it wholeheartedly.

My mum, Gloria Douglas, who gave me the freedom to explore who I really am and how I want to express myself, along with the resilience and independence to do it my way. And to my dad, Hugh Raper, who, throughout his fifteen-year journey with dementia and his death, taught me so much about being present, compassionate, and patient, and who showed me that life is so much more than what we see, it's what we feel.

My husband, Anthony Esselmont, for providing unconditional love and support and taking care of our two daughters, Chloe and Zara, so I could write my heart out.

All the people I have interacted with over the course of my life so far. Each and every person has offered me a lesson that has made me into who I am now.

Our Biddy Tarot tribe—people who I may never have seen in person, but have met through my courses, digital products, community, and website. These people have invited me into their lives to show them the true potential of the Tarot and, more importantly, the true potential of themselves.

And finally, I offer my gratitude to *you*. You have invited me into your life at this very moment, to guide you toward your inner wisdom, your inner power, and your intuition. And for that, I am truly grateful.

New Moon Visualization

CLOSE YOUR EYES AND TAKE IN A DEEP, CLEANSING BREATH. Feel your breath flowing down into your body, and as you exhale, feel your body gently relax.

Take another deep breath in, and as you breathe out, just let go and release any excess energy.

Take one more deep breath in. And this time as you breathe out, allow yourself to receive.

In this beautifully relaxed state, reconnect with your spirit, your source energy.

Call in your guides to be present and hold space for you.

Visualize a beautiful sacred circle around you, holding you and nurturing you. It might be a crystal grid, a circle of light, or even flowers and leaves that you have collected.

Now bring your attention to your heart. Imagine a beautiful, golden ball of light in your heart. Radiate that light throughout your whole body, filling every cell with radiant golden light.

Connect with Mother Earth, feeling your energy flowing down into the earth and feeling her energy flowing back up through your feet and your legs, grounding you into this sacred space.

Now, connect with the Universe and the Universal consciousness. Feel its bright light showering down on you, filling you with this pure source energy.

Imagine yourself at the beginning of a forest path. The trees are standing tall around you, and the late afternoon sun is shining through the leafy canopy. Start to walk down this path, and as you breathe in, you smell earthiness of the forest floor and the aroma of the leaves around you. Keep walking along the path, and as the sun begins to set, you can hear birds and wildlife around you.

Continue walking until eventually you reach a clearing. It's a lush, grassy field with wildflowers bursting from the ground. Find a comfortable place to sit, and as you do, you feel the presence of your guides around you, protecting you and nurturing you.

As the sun sets, you start to notice the stars shining brightly all around you.

As you look up into the night's sky, you notice a tiny sliver of the new moon.

Imagine the moon's energy as a silvery river of light flowing toward you from the sky.

Feel the new beginnings and opportunities flowing down to you.

Open up to receive any intuitive messages or visions that come through to you at this time as you sit under the new moon.

Reach into your pocket and, inside, you find a handful of seeds. Each of these seeds represents your intentions for this lunar cycle. Hold the seeds in your hand, then plant each seed into the ground.

Imagine the flow of the new moon energy coming down into the ground, filling your intentions with life force and energy, creating new life.

Feel the motivation, the energy, and the inspiration to manifest these intentions.

Feel the joy within you, as you prepare to take action to bring these intentions to life.

And feel the power within you growing and filling every cell within your body.

You are setting forth your intentions, putting them out in the world and taking action to manifest your goals and dreams.

Trust yourself and follow your instincts, knowing that you are doing important work.

Bless the new opportunities and new beginnings that are available to you now.

And bless the dreams of others, knowing that everyone can have what they truly desire.

Harness this powerful new energy and allow this energy to bless all people of the earth in the most graceful way.

Start to bring your awareness back into your body. Breathe in deeply, becoming aware of the space around you.

Move your toes, your feet, your hands, gently easing back into the present moment. And gently open your eyes.

Trust that all that is unfolding is in accordance with Divine Will. So be it.

Full Moon Visualization

Close your eyes and take in a deep, cleansing breath. Feel your breath flowing down into your body, and as you exhale, feel your body gently relax.

Take another deep breath in, and as you breathe out, just let go and release any excess energy.

Take one more deep breath in. And this time as you breathe out, allow yourself to receive.

In this beautifully relaxed state, reconnect with your spirit, your source energy.

Call in your guides to be present and hold space for you.

Visualize a beautiful sacred circle around you, holding you and nurturing you. It might be a crystal grid, a circle of light, or even flowers and leaves that you have collected.

Now bring your attention to your heart. Imagine a beautiful, golden ball of light in your heart. Radiate that light throughout your whole body, filling every cell with radiant golden light.

Connect with Mother Earth, feeling your energy flowing down into the earth and feeling her energy flowing back up through your feet and your legs, grounding you into this sacred space.

Now, connect with the Universe and the Universal consciousness. Feel its bright light showering down on you, filling you with this pure source energy.

Imagine yourself standing in a forest at nighttime. The trees are standing tall around you and the light from the full moon is filtering down through the leaves and bathing the forest in a beautiful silvery light.

You find yourself on a path and you begin to walk down this path, step by step. As you walk, you breathe in and smell earthiness of the forest floor and the aroma of the leaves around you.

You continue walking until you reach a clearing. You step into this clearing and stand under the moonlight. Feel the magical energy of the moon as it shines down on you. Bathe in this sacred feminine energy.

As you stand here, take a moment to give thanks for everything you have created since the last new moon.

{pause}

Ahead of you, you notice a large campfire around which people have gathered. You start to walk toward the fire and as you get closer, the fire guardian comes to meet and welcome you. The guardian is holding a smudge stick and gently waves the smoke over the front and the back of your body. The guardian then invites you into the circle around the campfire.

As you look into the fire, you become aware of the rhythmic beat of the drum, lulling you into an even deeper state of relaxation.

The guardian invites you to think about that which no longer serves you—worries, relationships, habits, thoughts, addictions . . . Each thought becomes words on paper that you collect in your hand. Continue to ask yourself, *What no longer serves me? What do I need to release and let go of?*

{pause}

Take those pieces of paper and toss them into the fire. Watch the flames envelop the pieces of paper as they begin to burn.

You now join hands with the people next to you and slowly you begin to walk around the campfire. Together, you begin to chant, "I release that which no longer serves me. I release that which no longer serves me. I release that which no longer serves me."

Feel all the excess energy releasing into the fire, as you let go of what no longer serves you.

Eventually, the circle slows down, and you stand around the fire watching the flames get smaller and smaller. Soon the fire is nothing but a pile of ash, smoke gently rising into the air.

With the fire now out, you gaze upward towards the sky and become aware of the silvery light of the full moon.

Feel the divine feminine energy flowing down toward you, filling you with Universal light and unconditional love.

Feel the joy of having released everything that no longer serves you.

Feel a lightness in your heart as you open the way for new opportunities.

{pause}

And as you stand here under the light of the full moon, harness this powerful energy and allow this energy to radiate throughout every cell of your body.

{pause}

Start to bring your awareness back into your body. Breathe in deeply, becoming aware of the space around you.

Move your toes, your feet, your hands, gently easing back into the present moment. And gently open your eyes.

Trust that all that is unfolding is in accordance with Divine Will. So be it.

INDEX

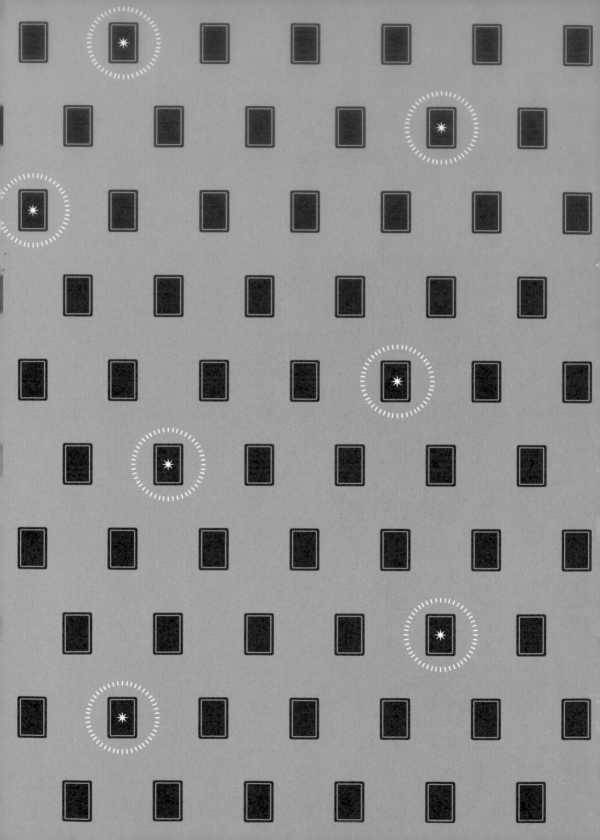